Effective Chinese Recipes

Compiled by   Tan Fenghua
              Tan Fengsen
              Tan Honghui
Translated by Yang Huiqin
              Cui Xiaohong
Revised by   Dwayne Walter

Shandong Science and Technology Press

First Edition 1996

Effective Chinese Recipes
Compiled by   Tan Fenghua, Tan Fengsen,
Tan Honghui
Translated by   Yang Huiqin, Cui Xiaohong
Revised by   Dwayne Walter
Published by Shandong Science and Technology Press
Printed by Foreign languages Printing House
Distributed by China International Book
Trading Corporation
35 Chegongzhuang Xilu, Beijing 100044, China

Printed in the People's Republic of China

PREFACE

Our father Tan Zhibin, a veteran TCM practioner of over 50 years of clinical experience, was born into a traditional doctor's family and he started his medical career when he was very young. He was taught by his father who passed on to him his treasured experience and family recipes. With his rich clinical experience, eagerness to learn from others and his creativity, Mr Tan enjoyed a high level of prestige among the people of his community by his uniqueness and flexibility in composing the drugs, and their remarkable effectiveness in treating miscellaneous difficult cases.

Among the prescriptions selected in this book, some are his family's secret recipes handed down for generations. Most are from Mr. Tan's treasured experience accumulated through his over half a century's clinical practice. Characterized by simplicity in the composition of recipes, convenience in the preparation of the drugs and reliability of the effectiveness, the book undoubtedly provides the TCM practitioners working in the country or mountionous areas with a good reference of TCM. It also provides the researchers of TCM with valuable material for promoting traditional Chinese medicine.

Owing to the limitation of our learning and understanding, Mr. Tan's experience may not be reached fully and correctly, so we sincerely expect the criticisms from our colleagues and experts.

Compilers

Contents

1. Internal Medicine

1.1. Common Cold ... 1
1.1.1. Decoction for Common Cold ... 1
1.1.2. Millet Decoction ... 1
1.1.3. Quick-acting Decoction for Common Cold ... 1
1.1.4. Decoction of Herba Elsholtziae seu Moslae and Bamboo Leaves ... 2
1.1.5. Decoction of Herba Artemisiae Chinghao ... 2
1.1.6. Powder of Pericarpium Citri Reticulatae ... 2
1.1.7. Powder for Common Cold of All Seasons ... 3
1.1.8. Pill for Cold and Headache ... 3

1.2. Heatstroke ... 4
1.2.1. Cooling Powder ... 4
1.2.2. Life-restoring Powder ... 4

1.3. Cough and Asthma ... 4
1.3.1. Powder for Cough and Asthma ... 4
1.3.2. Decoction for Relieving Cough and Asthma ... 5
1.3.3. Semi-fluid Extract for Intractable Cough ... 5
1.3.4. Cough-relieving Powder ... 5
1.3.5. Asthma-soothing Powder of Semen Ginkgo and Lumbricus ... 6
1.3.6. Asthma-relieving Paste ... 6
1.3.7. Gecko Bolus ... 7

1.4. Headache ... 7
1.4.1. Powder for Headache due to Wind-heat Evil ... 7
1.4.2. Powder for Headache due to Blood-stasis ... 7
1.4.3. Powder for Relieving Headache by Regulating Collaterals ... 8
1.4.4. Powder for Migraine and Headache ... 8

1.4.5. Medicated Hen Soup ········· 8
1.4.6. Quick-acting Powder for Headache ········· 9
1.4.7. Powder of Rhizoma Gastrodiae for Soothing Migraine ········· 9
1.4.8. Decoctoin for Clearing Away Headache ········· 9
1.4.9. Decoction for Expelling Migraine and Overall Headache ········· 10

1.5. *Dizziness* ········· 11
1.5.1. Powder for Stopping Dizziness ········· 11
1.5.2. Pillow for Clearing Head and Neck Ailment ········· 11
1.5.3. Decoction for Nourishing Blood ········· 11

1.6. *Hysteria* ········· 12
1.6.1. Powder for Treating Hysteria ········· 12
1.6.2. Decoction of Fructus Tritici Levis ········· 12
1.6.3. Decoction of Nardostachyos and Pericarpium Citri Reticulatae ········· 12

1.7. *Epilepsy and Mania* ········· 13
1.7.1. Heart-soothing Pill for Mania ········· 13
1.7.2. Medicated Soup of Owl and Lamb Heart ········· 13
1.7.3. Placenta Bolus ········· 14

1.8. *Insomnia* ········· 14
1.8.1. Sleeping Pill ········· 14
1.8.2. Egg Decoction for Insomnia ········· 14

1.9. *Hypertension* ········· 15
1.9.1. Antihypertensive Bolus ········· 15
1.9.2. Antihypertensive Decoction ········· 15
1.9.3. Bolus for Treating Hypertension and Dizziness ········· 16
1.9.4. Food of Six Red Ingredients for Lowering High Blood Pressure ········· 16

1.10. *Deviation of the Eye and Mouth* ········· 17
1.10.1. Honey Locust and Vinegar Lotion ········· 17
1.10.2. Plaster for Correcting Deviation ········· 17
1.10.3. Cottonseed Bolus ········· 18

1.11. *Apoplexy* ········· 18

1.11.1. Scolopendra Powder ... 18
1.11.2. Bolus for Treating Apoplexy I ... 18
1.11.3. Bolus for Treating Apoplexy II ... 19
1.12. *Numbness (Appendix: Pain of the Waist and Leg)* ... 20
1.12.1. Egg Shell Powder ... 20
1.12.2. Wine Medicated with Scorpio and Fructus Chaenomelis ... 20
1.12.3. Tendon-relaxing Lotion ... 20
1.12.4. Powder for Relieving Pain of the Waist and Legs ... 21
1.12.5. Decoction for Treating "Bi Syndrome" ... 22
1.12.6. Semen Strychni Pill ... 22
1.13. *Night Sweat* ... 23
1.13.1. Sweat-stopping Decoction ... 23
1.13.2. Powder for Treating Night Sweat ... 23
1.13.3. Decoction for Postpartum Sweating ... 23
1.14. *Stomachache* ... 24
1.14.1. Pill for Stomachache ... 24
1.14.2. Powder of Os Sepiellae seu Sepiae and Peanuts ... 24
1.14.3. Powder of Three Burnt Ingredients ... 24
1.14.4. Powder of Cuttlebone and Evodia Fruit ... 25
1.14.5. Powder for Relieving Three Pains ... 25
1.14.6. Stomach-soothing Powder ... 25
1.15. *Diarrhea (Appendix: Dysentery)* ... 26
1.15.1. Powder for Stopping Diarrhea ... 26
1.15.2. Gruel of Rhizoma Dioscoreae for Stopping Diarrhea ... 26
1.15.3. Pill for Stopping Diarrhea and for Reinforcing Rectum ... 27
1.15.4. Antidiarrheal Lotion ... 27
1.15.5. Pill for Arresting Dysentery ... 27
1.15.6. Powder for Treating Dysentery with Pus and Blood ... 28
1.15.7. Powder for Treating Bloody Dysentery ... 28
1.15.8. Bark and Peel Powder ... 29

1.15.9. Powder of Three Burnt Ingredients ················· 29
1.16. *Hepatitis (Appendix : Jaundice)* ················· 29
1.16.1. Bolus for Treating Acute Icterohepatitis ················· 29
1.16.2. Decoction for Soothing the Liver ················· 29
1.16.3. Jaundice-relieving Bolus ················· 30
1.16.4. Herba Artemisiae Scopariae Decoction for Treating Jaundice ················· 30
1.17. *Constipation (Appendix : Bloody Stool)* ················· 31
1.17.1. Decoction for Moistening Intestines ················· 31
1.17.2. Semifluid Extract for Moistening Intestines ················· 31
1.17.3. Bowel-relaxing Suppository ················· 31
1.17.4. Cortex Ailanthi Bolus for Arresting Blood ················· 32
1.17.5. Decoction for Treating Bloody Stool ················· 32
1.18. *Dysuria* ················· 32
1.18.1. Decoction for Relieving Dysuria ················· 32
1.18.2. Powder for Restoring Normal Urination ················· 33
1.18.3. Medulla Junci Decoction ················· 33
1.19. *Hiccup* ················· 33
1.19.1. Decoction of Calyx Kaki ················· 33
1.19.2. Cigarette of Realgar and Nails ················· 34
1.19.3. Powder of Gallbladder and Semen Litchi ················· 34
1.19.4. Decoction for Treating Hiccup due to Qi Obstruction ················· 34
1.20. *Vomiting* ················· 34
1.20.1. Pill for Stopping Vomiting ················· 34
1.20.2. Powder for Treating Vomiting I ················· 35
1.20.3. Powder for Treating Vomiting II ················· 35
1.20.4. Decoction for Treating Abdominal Pain and Vomiting ················· 36
1.20.5. Decoction for Arresting Vomiting ················· 36
1.20.6. Ochra Powder ················· 37
1.21. *Dysphagia* ················· 37
1.21.1. Bolus for Stopping Dysphagia and Globus Hystericus ················· 37
1.21.2. Powder of Baby Mice ················· 37

1.21.3. Decoction for Dysphagia and Regurgitation ·············· 38
1.22. *Pain in the Chest and Hypochondria* ················ 38
1.22.1. Qi-regulating Pill of Jujube ························· 38
1.22.2. Juice of Fragrant-flowered Garlic ···················· 39
1.22.3. Decoction for Promoting Qi Circulation ············· 39
1.23. *Stranguria* ··· 40
1.23.1. Pill for Relieving Five Kinds of Stranguria ········· 40
1.23.2. Semifluid Extract for Treating Stranguria ··········· 41
1.24. *Diabetes* ··· 41
1.24.1. Diabetes-relieving Bolus ··························· 41
1.24.2. Gruel of Rhizoma Dioscoreae and Cucurbita
        Moschata ··· 41
1.25. *Enuresis* ··· 42
1.25.1. Powder of Rooster's Intestines ····················· 42
1.25.2. Decoction for Treating Enuresis ····················· 42
1.25.3. Decoction for Avoiding Bed-wetting ················· 43
1.26. *Hernia* ··· 43
1.26.1. Powder for Treating Hernia ························· 43
1.26.2. Bolus for Treating Hernia ·························· 44
1.26.3. Powder of Scolopendra ····························· 44
1.27. *Nocturnal Emission* ·································· 44
1.27.1. Pill for Treating Nocturnal Emission ··············· 44
1.27.2. Powder for Stopping Nocturnal Emission ············· 45
1.27.3. Bolus of Sparrow Eggs and Semen Allri Tuberosi ····· 45
1.28. *Impotence* ·· 45
1.28.1. Yang-restoring Powder ····························· 45
1.28.2. Medicated Wine for Treating Impotence ············· 46
1.28.3. Snail Powder for Treating Impotence ··············· 46
1.28.4. Yang-reinforcing Decoction ························ 46
1.29. *Sterility Due to Deficiency of Sperms* ·············· 46
1.29.1. Powder of Rehmanniae and Dioscoreae ··············· 46
1.29.2. Sperm-producing Bolus ····························· 47

1.30. *Constriction of Penis (Appendix: Priapism)* ········ 47
1.30.1. A Combined Recipe for Treating Constriction of Penis ········ 47
1.30.2. Decoction for Relieving Priapism ········ 48

2. Surgery

2.1. *Acute Mastitis* ········ 49
2.1.1. Paste for Relieving Acute Mastitis ········ 49
2.1.2. Mirabilitum Mixture ········ 49
2.1.3. Paste for Relieving Mammary Abscess ········ 49
2.1.4. Fructus Trichosanthes Decoction ········ 50
2.1.5. Abscess-relieving Decoction ········ 50
2.2. *Pyogenic Infection and Ulcerous Disease of Skin* ······ 51
2.2.1. Powder for Relieving Ulcerous Disease of Skin ········ 51
2.2.2. Five-twig Ointment for Restoring Yang ········ 51
2.2.3. Ointment for Treating Carbuncles Around the Shoulder Blade ········ 52
2.2.4. Paste for Malignant Lentigo ········ 52
2.3. *Pustule of the Finger Tip* ········ 53
2.3.1. Pustule-curing Egg ········ 53
2.3.2. Pustule-curing Ointment ········ 53
2.4. *Furuncle (Appendix: Inflammatory Disease With Redness of Skin* ········ 53
2.4.1. Ointment for Treating Furuncle ········ 53
2.4.2. Anti-toxic Decoction ········ 54
2.4.3. Five-twig Ointment ········ 54
2.4.4. Chrysanthemum Decoction ········ 54
2.4.5. Yellow Powder ········ 55
2.4.6. Decoction of Periostracum Cicadae and Two Kinds of Flowers ········ 55
2.5. *Carbuncle on the Back or on the Nape* ········ 55
2.5.1. Powder for Removing Rotten Tissure ········ 55

2.5.2. Powder of Resina Olibani and Radix et Rhizoma Rhei
(Appendix: Bile and Ink Paste) ·· 56
2.5.3. Carbuncle-curing Lotion ·· 56
2.6. Scrofula ·· 56
2.6.1. Scrofula-treating Lotion of Spiders ································ 56
2.6.2. Scolopendra Powder ·· 57
2.6.3. Suppositories Made of Donkey-hide Gelatin ··············· 57
2.7. Small Boils Near the Hairline ·· 58
2.7.1. Earthen Vat Powder ·· 58
2.7.2. Three Ashes Plaster ·· 58
2.7.3. Herba Equiseti Hiemalis Plaster ··································· 58
2.8. Pustulosis Bullous ··· 59
2.8.1. Realgar Powder ·· 59
2.8.2. Powder of Exocarpium Citrulli ······································ 59
2.8.3. Powder of Indigo Naturalis and Cortex Phellodendri ············ 59
2.9. Ecthyma ·· 60
2.9.1. Ecthyma Plaster ··· 60
2.9.2. Hair Powder ·· 60
2.9.3. Convenient Ointment ··· 60
2.10. Scrofula Around the Neck ··· 61
2.10.1. Powder of Realgar and Gecko ····································· 61
2.10.2. Calx Powder (Appendix: Herba Erodiiseu Geranii) ············ 61
2.11. Scaby Head ··· 62
2.11.1. Powder for Scaby Head ··· 62
2.11.2. Ointment for White Ringworm ····································· 62
2.12. Alopecia Areata ··· 62
2.12.1. Powder for Alopecia Areata ··· 62
2.12.2. Hair-growing Bolus ··· 63
2.12.3. Semen Strychni Oil ··· 63
2.13. Scabies ··· 64
2.13.1. Tadpole Drink ·· 64
2.13.2. Sulfur Lotion ·· 64

2.13.3. Folium Typhonii Lotion 64
2.14. *Tinea* (*Appendix*: *Goose Foot Tinea*) 65
2.14.1. Natrii Sulfas Ointment 65
2.14.2. Alumen Powder 65
2.14.3. Ointment for Tinea 65
2.14.4. Hand-soaking Lotion (Appendix: Semen Strychni Oil) 66
2.15. *Intertrigo Eczema Behind the Ear* 66
2.15.1. Powder for Ear Eczema(Appendix: Cortex
    Phellodendri Powder) 66
2.16. *Fire Burn and Scald* 67
2.16.1. Ointment for Fire Burn and Scald(Appendix:
    Recipe I, II) 67
2.17. *Vitiligo* 68
2.17.1. Powder for Vitiligo 68
2.17.2. Mylabris Lotion 68
2.18. *Acne* 68
2.18.1. Decoction for Acne 68
2.18.2. Acne Cream 69
2.19. *Paronychia* 69
2.19.1. Rhizoma Rhei Powder 69
2.19.2. Pollen Powder of Typhonii 69
2.20. *Tetanus* 70
2.20.1. Powder for Treating Tetanus 70
2.20.2. Decoction of Periostracum Cicadae 70
2.20.3. Decoction for Expelling the Wind Evil 70
2.21. *Corn* 71
2.21.1. Corn-removing Paste 71
2.21.2. Powder of Calx and Alkaline 71
2.22. *Wart* 71
2.22.1. Lotion of Kelp and Rhizoma Cyperi 71
2.23. *Itch & Swell of Scrotum* 72
2.23.1 Wash Lotion for Scrotum Ailment 72

2.24. *Chilblain* ………………………………………………… 72
2.24.1. Powder of Freshwater Mussel Shell ………………… 72
2.25. *Appendicitis* ……………………………………………… 73
2.25.1. Decoction for Treating Appendicitis ……………………… 73

3. Gynecology

3.1. *Amenorrhea* ……………………………………………… 74
3.1.1. Decoction of Radix Angelicae Sinenisis ………………… 74
3.1.2. Pill of Three Yellow Ingredients for Restoring Menstruation ………………………………………………… 74
3.1.3. Pill for Treating Amenorrhea ……………………………… 75
3.2. *Dysmenorrhea* ……………………………………………… 75
3.2.1. Decoction for Relieving Pain During Menstruation ……… 75
3.2.2. Herba Leonuri Pill ………………………………………… 75
3.2.3. Decoction for Expelling Cold Invasion Prior to Menstruation ………………………………………………… 76
3.3. *Retrograde Menstruation* ………………………………… 76
3.3.1. Decoction for Retrograde Menstruation ………………… 76
3.3.2. Powder for Perverse Flow of Menses …………………… 77
3.3.3. Os Draconis Powder for Stopping Bleeding (Appendix: Decoction of Four Fresh Ingredients) ……………………… 77
3.4. *Uterine Bleeding* …………………………………………… 78
3.4.1. Decoction for Treating Uterine Bleeding by Strengthening Qi …………………………………………… 78
3.4.2. Powder for Consolidating Blood ………………………… 78
3.4.3. Powder of Three Carbonized Ingredients ……………… 78
3.4.4. Powder of Herba Cephalanoploris ……………………… 79
3.5. *Leucorrhagia* ……………………………………………… 79
3.5.1. Decoction for Treating Leucorrhagia …………………… 79
3.5.2. Powder for Treating Leucorrhagia ……………………… 80
3.5.3. Egg of Semen Ginkgo and Fructus Piperis Nigri ……… 80
3.6. *Morning Sickness* ………………………………………… 80

3.6.1. Fructus Mume Decoction ······ 80
3.6.2. Drink of Terra Flava Usta ······ 81
3.7. *Fetus-soothing* ······ 81
3.7.1. Fetus-soothing Decoction ······ 81
3.7.2. Powder for Treating Threatened Abortion ······ 82
3.8. *Frequent Urination During Pregnancy (Appendix: Dysuria)* ······ 82
3.8.1. Folium Kochiae Decoction ······ 82
3.9. *Postpartum Abdominal Pain* ······ 82
3.9.1. Powder for Relieving Abdominal Pain ······ 82
3.9.2. Decoction for Warming the Meridians to Relieve Pain ······ 83
3.10. *Postpartum Faintness* ······ 83
3.10.1. Quick-acting Powder for Postpartum Faintness (Appendix) ······ 83
3.10.2. Drink of Cinnabaris and Baby's Urine ······ 84
3.11. *Promoting Lactation (Appendix: Lactifuge)* ······ 84
3.11.1. Pig's Trotter Soup for Promoting Lactation ······ 84
3.11.2. Powder of Squama Manitis and Colla Cornus Cervis (Appendix: Recipe Ⅰ, Ⅱ) ······ 84
3.11.3. Malt Decoction for Lactifuge ······ 85
3.12. *Pruritus Vulvae* ······ 85
3.12.1. Five Leaves Washing Lotion ······ 85

4. Paediatrics

4.1. *Infantile Malnutrition* ······ 86
4.1.1. Powder for Treating Infantile Malnutrition ······ 86
4.1.2. Nutrition-improving Powder ······ 86
4.1.3. Baby-soothing Pill ······ 87
4.2. *Infantile Convulsion* ······ 87
4.2.1. Powder for Treating Convulsion ······ 87
4.2.2. Powder for Expelling Wind Evil ······ 88
4.2.3. Convulsion-preventing Powder ······ 88

4.3. *Neonatal Tetanus* ……… 88
4.3.1. Powder for Treating Neonatal Tetanus ……… 88
4.4. *Morbid Night Crying of a Baby* ……… 89
4.4.1. Decoction for Stopping Night Crying Recipe I ……… 89
4.4.2. Decoction for Stopping Night Crying Recipe II ……… 89
4.5. *Whooping Cough* ……… 89
4.5.1. Whooping Cough Oil ……… 89
4.5.2. Powder of Chicken Gallbladder and Radix Glycyrrhizae ……… 90
4.5.3. Flos Genkwa Pill ……… 90
4.5.4. Cough-relieving Powder for Children ……… 90
4.6. *Measles* ……… 91
4.6.1. Powder for Promoting Eruption of Measles ……… 91
4.6.2. Powder for Clearing Away Fever ……… 92
4.6.3. Decoction for Promoting Eruption of Measles ……… 92
4.7. *Infantile Parasitosis* ……… 93
4.7.1. Decoction of Fructus Quisqualis and Cortex Meliae ……… 93
4.7.2. Pinworm-expelling Powder ……… 93
4.7.3. Pill of Green Vitriol and Fructus Quisqualis ……… 93
4.8. *Infantile Diarrhea* ……… 94
4.8.1. Powder for Stopping Diarrhea ……… 94
4.9. *Infantile Abdominal Pain* (*Appendix*: *Abdominal Distension*) ……… 94
4.9.1. Powder for Abdominal Pain in Children ……… 94
4.10. *Prolapse of Rectum in Children* ……… 95
4.10.1. Powder for Treating Prolapse of Rectum ……… 95
4.10.2. Decoction of Radix Astragali seu Hedysari ……… 95
4.11. *Omphalelcosis* ……… 96
4.11.1. Powder for Treating Omphalelcosis ……… 96
4.12. *Boil of the Chin in Children* ……… 96
4.12.1. Ointment of Carbonized Dates ……… 96
4.13. *Fetal Toxins* ……… 97
4.13.1. Ointment for Treating Fetal Toxins (Appendix) ……… 97

4.13.2. Decoction of Flos Trollii and Radix Rehmanniae ········· 97
4.14. *Mumps* ········· 97
4.14.1. Powder for Treating Mumps(Appendix) ········· 97
4.15. *Heat Rash* ········· 98
4.15.1. Powder of Mung Bean and Talcum (Appendix) ········· 98

5. Department of the Five-sense Organs

5.1. *Ophthalmology* ········· 99
5.1.1. Sight-recovering Decoction ········· 99
5.1.2. Nebula-expelling Decoction ········· 99
5.1.3. Nebula-expelling Powder ········· 99
5.1.4. Trichiasis-adjusting Ointment ········· 100
5.2. *Otopathy* ········· 100
5.2.1. Powder of Cow Gallbladder and Mung Beans ········· 100
5.3. *Rhinitis* ········· 100
5.3.1. Semi-fluid Extract for Treating Rhinitis ········· 100
5.3.2. Powder for Treating Rhinitis ········· 101
5.4. *Sore Throat* ········· 101
5.4.1. Sore Throat Drink ········· 101
5.4.2. Powder for Pharyngitis ········· 102
5.4.3. Powder for Throat Ailments ········· 102
5.4.4. Voice-recovering Drink ········· 103
5.5. *Mouth Cavity Ailment* ········· 103
5.5.1. Powder of Fructus Euodiae and Water-melon Frost ········· 103
5.5.2. Ache-relieving Powder ········· 103
5.5.3. Colophonium Paste ········· 104
5.5.4. Quick-acting Powder for Toothache ········· 104
5.5.5. Ten Ingredients Decoction for Treating Toothache ········· 104

6. Others

6.1. *Medicinal Wine for Trauma* ········· 106
6.2. *Black Plaster* ········· 106

6.3. Resuscitation Powder 107
6.4. Nightmare-Expelling Decoction 108
6.5. Sleeping Decoction 108
6.6. Wonder Pill 109
6.7. Pill of Strychni and Lumbricus 109
6.8. Spider Ointment 110
6.9. Bolus for Treating Consumption 110
6.10. Pain-Relieving Powder 111
6.11. Stye-Dispersing Paste 111
6.12. Pain-Relieving Decoction 111
6.13. Semen Lotion 112
6.14. Plaster for Hyperplasia of Bones 112

1. Internal Medicine

1.1. Common Cold

1.1.1. Decoction for Common Cold

Indications: Invasion of pathogenic wind-cold evil in winter, with symptoms like headache, fever, aversion to cold. There is also no perspiration.

Prescription: Chinese cabbage root (cleaned) 1 Piece, fibrous roots of Chinese onion 5 Pcs, Rhizoma Zingiberis Recens 3 Pcs.

Administration: Make a glass of decoction with the above ingredients to be taken hot so that there will be a little perspiration.

1.1.2. Millet Decoction

Indications: Common cold in winter and spring with such symptoms as fever, headache, general soreness and weakness.

Prescription: Millet 50g, Folium Mori (frost-beaten) 10g, Cacumen Tamaricis 15g.

Administration: Make one glass of decoction to be taken hot, covered in quilt to perspire a little.

1.1.3. Quick-acting Decoction for Common Cold

Indications: Cold, fever and headache.

Prescription: Radix Ledebouriellae 10g, Rhizoma Ligustici Chuanxiong 10g, Radix Scutellariae 10g, Herba Asari 3g, Rhizoma Atractylodis 9g, Rhizoma seu Radix Notopterygii

1

6g, Radix Angelicae Dahuricae 9g, Radix Bupleuri 9g, Radix Rehmannia 18g.

Administration: Decoct the above ingredients twice and then put the two decoctions together. The remedy should be taken half in the morning, half in the evening. Usually 1~2 day's medication will bring about a cure.

1.1.4. Decoction of Herba Elsholtziae seu Moslae and Bamboo Leaves

Indications: Cold in summer with symptoms like fever, heavy feeling in the head, tight chest, weak limbs and occasional diarrhea.

Prescription: Herba Elsholtziae seu Moslae 9g, Cortex Magnoliae Officinalis 9g, bamboo leaves 4.5g, Semen Dolichoris Album 15g.

Administration: Make a decoction of the above ingredients, Take half the decoction each time.

1.1.5. Decoction of Herba Artemisiae Chinghao

Indications: Onset of cold with fever and headache, dry and sore throat.

Prescription: Herba Artemisiae Chinghao 10g, Radix Ophiopogonis 10g, Rhizoma Imperatae 30g, Rhizoma Phragmitis (fresh) 30g.

Administration: Decoct the above ingredients twice and then put the decoctions together. The remedy should be taken 3 times.

1.1.6. Powder of Pericarpium Citri Reticulatae

Indications: Cold with cough, stuffiness in the chest and costal regions, and loss of appetite.

Prescription: Pericarpium Citri Reticulatae 100g, Rhizoma Pinelliae 60g, Herba Coriandri Sativi (dried) 90g, cabbage roots(dried)100g.

Administration: Grind the above ingredients into a powder and then take 10~15g with sugar and water 3 times per day.

1.1.7. Powder for Common Cold of All Seasons

Indications: High fever due to invasion of exogenic factors, complicated by cough, blocked nose with clear nasal discharge, general soreness and heaviness of the body, abdominal distension, aversion to food and, in some cases night sweat. The remedy can also promote the onset of measles.

Prescription: Herba Menthae, Folium Perillae, Herba Schizomepetae, Radix Bupleuri, Radix Puerariae, Radix Scutellariae, Semen pruni Armeniacae, Cortex Magnoliae Officinalis and Fructus Tsaoko 10g each; Semen Coicis 20g, Semen Arecae (stir-fried) 6g, medicated leaven 6g, Fructus Crataegi 6g, Fructus Hordei Germinatus 6g, Herba Ephedrae 4.5g, Folium Sennae 2g.

Administration: Make a fine powder of the above ingredients. Store the powder in a bottle. An infant younger than 3 months can take 0.3g per time, between 3 months and 1 year 0.3~1g, 1~6 years 1~1.5g, 6~12 years 1.5~2g, above 12 years and adults can take 2~3g with a little sugar and water, 3 times a day.

1.1.8. Pill for Cold and Headache

Indications: Common cold, headache.

Prescription: Radix Ledebouriellae 500g, Radix Scutellariae 500g, Rhizoma seu Radix Noto-pterygii 500g, Radix Angelicae Dahuricae 500g, Rhizoma Ligustici 300g, Herba Schizonepetae 300g, Rhizoma Ligustici Chuanxiong 300g, Herba Asari 200g.

Administration: Grind the above ingredients to a fine powder and mix it with water to make pills of mung beans size. The medicine should be taken in doses 6~9g 3 times a day with plain water.

Note: The pills are also effective against chronic headache. A reduced dosage is recommended if there are side effects like a dry throat or excessive perspiration.

1.2. Heatstroke
1.2.1. Cooling Powder
Indications: Summer time dizziness, headache, restlessness, nausea and vomiting due to excess heat.

Prescription: Gypsum Fibrosum 60g, Talcum 60g, Herba Menthae(crystalized)3g, Fructus Mume 3g, Cinnabaris (prepared with water)6g, Radix Glycyrrhizae(powder)30g.

Administration: Grind the above ingredients to a fine powder and store it in a bottle. The remedy should be taken in doses 6g each time with cold water.

1.2.2. Life-restoring Powder
Indications: Loss of consciousness due to heatstroke in summer.

Prescription: Fructus Gleditsiae Abnormalis 10g, Herba Asari 10g, Realgar 2g, Borneolum Syntheticum 1g, Moschus 0.2g.

Administration: Grind the above ingredients to a fine powder, then store and seal it in a bottle. Take a tiny portion and blow the powder into the patient's nostrils, the patient will regain his or her consciousness instantly.

1.3. Cough and Asthma
1.3.1. Powder for Cough and Asthma
Indications: Intractable cough with phlegm and restlessness.

Prescription: Semen Raphani (stir-fried) 60g, Semen Juglandis (baked)100g, Semen pruni Armeniacae(stir-fried, skin and tips removed)100g, Bulbus Fritillariae Cirrhosae 60g, Semen Ziziphi Spinosae(stir-fried)30g.

Administration: Grind the above ingredients to a powder, take 6g each time with crystal sugar and water, twice a day.

1.3.2. Decoction for Relieving Cough and Asthma

Indications: Chronic bronchitis, asthma, cough.

Prescription: Semen Lepidii seu Descurainiae 9g, Cortex Mori Radicis 9g, Semen Ginkgo 9g, Semen pruni Armeniacae(stir-fried)9g, Rhizoma Pinelliae 6g, Radix Scutellariae 6g, Radix Asparagi 6g, Radix Glycyrrhizae(prepared)6g.

Administration: Make a decoction of the above ingredients. Take half decoction in the morning, half in the evening.

Caution: Raw, cold, oily, heavy and spicy food should be avoided.

1.3.3. Semi-fluid Extract for Intractable Cough

Indications: Intractable cough in the elderly complicated with coughing up phlegm, short breath and dyspnea.

Prescription: Semen Juglandis 120g, big pears(peeled and cores removed) 2 Pcs, fresh ginger (peeled) 120g, crystal sugar 120g, honey 250g, sesame oil 250g.

Administration: First pound Semen Juglandis, fresh ginger and pears into a paste. Then boil it with sugar and honey for 15 minutes. Afterwards add sesame oil and stew it till the semi-fluid turns brown. Store the paste in a porcelain jar. Take 15g 3 times a day with boiled water.

1.3.4. Cough-relieving Powder

Indications: Cough with retention of phlegm.

Prescription: Semen pruni Armeniacae(stir-fried, peeled) 12g, Cortex Mori Radicis(processed with honey)12g, Pericarpium

Citri Reticulatae 12g, Rhizoma Pinelliae 9g, Herba Asari 9g, Radix Stemonae 9g, Bulbus Fritillariae Cirrhosae 10g, Folium Perillae 10g, Radix Peucedani 10g, Gypsum Fibrosum 10g, Radix Glycyrrhizae 10g, Herba Ephedrae 6g, Semen Lepidii seu Descurainiae 6g, Poria 15g, Rhizoma Zingiberis 6g.

Administration: Grind the above ingredients to a fine powder and then store it in a bottle. Take the powder 3 times a day in doses of 3g after mixing it with sugar and water.

Note: This recipe includes drugs of both cold and warm nature. A better effect can be achieved when it is used to treat cough induced by cold.

1.3.5. Asthma-soothing Powder of Semen Ginkgo and Lumbricus

Indications: Asthma.

Prescription: Semen Ginkgo (smashed and baked yellow on a tile) 60g, Lumbricus (stir-fried) 60g, Semen Lepidii seu Descurainiae (stir-fried) 30g.

Administration: Grind the above ingredients to a fine powder and then store it in a bottle. Take the remedy 2~3 times a day in doses of 6~9g after mixing it with crystal sugar and water. A reduced dose for children is recommened.

1.3.6. Asthma-relieving Paste

Indications: Long-standing or recent asthmatic cough and asthma.

Prescription: Semen Momordicae 60g, Semen Pharbitidis (dark-colored) 15g, (white-colored) 15g, white pepper 7 Pcs, 4 eggs laid by a white hen.

Administration: Pound the first four ingredients and mix them well with the egg whites in order to make a paste. Apply the paste to Yongquan Point, use the left side for men and the right side for women. Wrap the foot with paper and stay in bed for 15 hours, then remove it. Apply it once every 7 days.

Note: Clinical applications in more than 100 cases proved that all the asthmatic patients were cured with 1~6 sessions of treatment.

1.3.7. Gecko Bolus

Indications: Long-standing cough with dyspnea, stuffiness in the chest, swollen face and extremities as well as fever accompanied with restlessness.

Prescription: Big Gecko (prepared) 2Pcs, Cortex Mori Radicis (prepared) 60g, Poria 60g, Radix Stephaniae Tetrandrae 45g, Semen Lepidii seu Descurainiae (stir-fried) 45g, Semen pruni Armeniacae (baked with tips removed) 45g, Caulis Akebiae 12g, Herba Ephedrae 30g, Pericarpium Citri Reticulatae 15g.

Administration: Grind the above ingredients into a fine powder, and mix it with processed honey in order to make boluses of 9g each. Take 1 bolus twice a day with a fresh ginger decoction.

1.4. *Headache*

1.4.1. Powder for Headache due to Wind-heat Evil

Indications: Headache due to wind-heat evil.

Prescription: Radix Angelicae Dahuricae 9g, Herba Schizonepetae 3g, Flos Chrysanthemi 6g, Rhizoma Gastrodiae 6g, Concha Haliotidis 10g.

Administration: Grind the above ingredients into a fine powder. Take twice a day 6g each time after mixing it with sugar and water.

1.4.2. Powder for Headache due to Blood-stasis

Indications: Headache due to blood-stasis resulted from a trauma.

Prescription: Radix Angelicae Sinensis 30g, Rhizoma Ligustici Chuanxiong 120g, Fructus Viticis 60g, Flos Carthami 20g, Radix Angelicae Dahuricae 24g.

Administration: Grind the ingredients to a fine powder. Take 6g each time after breakfast and supper with warm boiled water.

1.4.3. Powder for Relieving Headache by Regulating Collaterals

Indications: Long-standing nervous headache.

Prescription: Scorpio (stir-fried) 12g, Ramulus Uncariae cum Uncis 12g, Radix Glycyrrhizae 12g, Lumbricus (stir-fried) 9g, Herba Asari 3g.

Administration: Grind the above ingredients into a powder. Take 3g every morning and evening with warm boiled water.

1.4.4. Powder for Migraine and Headache

Indications: Migraine and headache

Prescription: Fructus Xanthii 100g, Radix Angelicae Dahuricae 20g.

Administration: Grind the above ingredients into a fine powder. Take 2g every morning and evening with warm boiled water.

Note: The above four recipes can be used flexibly in clinical applications. A better effect will be achieved if used coordinately.

1.4.5. Medicated Hen Soup

Indications: Headache, dizziness and long-standing migraine.

Prescription: Rhizoma Gastrodiae 45g, Radix Angelicae Dahuricae 10g, 1 hen.

Administration: Remove the hen's internal organs. Then put the other two ingredients into the abdominal region and sew it up, eat the hen soup twice a day after cooking it well. The soup should last 3 days.

1.4.6. Quick-acting Powder for Headache

Indications: Acute migraine or headache

Prescription: Flos Magnoline 5g, Semen Impatientis 5g, Herba Menthae(crystalized)1g, Borneolum Syntheticus 0.5g.

Administration: Grind the above ingredients into a fine powder. Inhale a tiny portion into the nostrils, use the right nostril for a left-side headache, and use the left for a right-side headache. If it is an overall headache, inhale the powder with both nostrils. The headache will be relieved instantly.

Note: Clinical applications to hundreds of cases show that this powder can soothe the pain very quickly.

1.4.7. Powder of Rhizoma Gastrodiae for Soothing Migraine

Indications: Migraine.

Prescription: Rhizoma Gastrodiae 10g, Radix Salviae Miltiorrhizae 10g, Ramulus Uncariae cum Uncis 10g, Rhizoma Ligustici 12g, Scorpio(stir-fried) 12g, Lumbricus(stir-fried) 12g.

Administration: Grind the above ingredients into a fine powder. Take 2~3g twice a day with warm boiled water.

1.4.8. Decoction for Clearing Away Headache

Indications: Headache, dizziness (caused by hypertension or cerebral concussion).

Prescription: Radix Angelicae Sinensis 12g, Radix Rehmannia 12g, Ramulus Uncariae cum Uncis 12g, Flos Chrysanthemi Indici 10g, Radix Platycodi 10g, Rhizoma Gastrodiae 10g, Cortex Eucommiae 10g, Herba Ecliptae 15g, Concha Ostreae 15g, Os Draconis 20g, Radix Polygalae 9g, Radix Glycyrrhizae 6g.

Administration: Decoct the above ingredients twice and mix the decoctions together. Take half of the mixture in the morning, half in the evening.

1.4.9. Decoction for Expelling Migraine and Overall Headache

Indications: All sorts of headaches.

Prescription: Radix Ophiopogonis 5g, Radix Scutellariae 4g, Rhizoma Seu Radix Noto-pterygii 3g, Radix Angelicae Pubescentis 3g, Radix Ledebouriellae 3g, Atractylodis 3g, Radix Angelicae Sinensis 3g, Rhizoma Ligustici 3g, Radix Angelicae Dahuricae 3g, Flos Chrysanthemi 2g, Fructus Viticis 2g, Herba Asari 1g, Radix Glycyrrhizae 1g, Rhizoma Zingiberis 0.5g.

Modification of the Prescription: Add Flos Carthami 2g, Radix Gentianae 2g, Radix Rehmanniae 2g and Radix Bupleuri 3g to the prescription for headache on the left; add Radix Astragali seu Hedysari 2g, Radix Puerariae 3g for headache on the right; if an acute pain occurs on the forehead, add Rhizoma Gastrodiae 2g, Fructus Aurantii Immaturus 2g, Rhizoma Pinelliae 3g and Fructus Crataegi 3g; if the Pain is in the top, add Rhizoma Ligustici 3g, Radix et Rhizoma Rhei 1g; if the pain is caused by invasion of wind-evil to the brains, add Fructus Xanthii 3g, Fructus Chaenomelis 2g, Herba Schizonepatae 2g; in cases of deficiency of energy and blood with night sweat and headache, add Radix Astragali seu Hedysari 3g, Radix Ginseng 3g, Radix Paeoniae Alba 3g, Radix Rehmannia 3g.

Administration: Decoct the above ingredients twice and mix the decoctions together. Take half in the morning, half in the evening.

Note: This ancient recipe is composed of drugs capable of dispelling wind, promoting blood circulation, regulating vital energy, eliminating fluid retention, removing blood stasis and endogenous cold-evil in the head. Therefore it is effective in treating wind-cold evil, stagnation of vital energy and blood, perverse flow of qi and water dampness in the head. Many years of clinical experience proves that the result is quite satisfactory if the ingredients are chosen flexibly.

1.5. Dizziness

1.5.1. Powder for Stopping Dizziness

Indications: Headache and dizziness.

Prescription: Semen Ginkgo (baked brown on a tile) 60g, Flos Althaeae Roseae (seeds removed, baked brown on a tile) 45g, Gypsum Fibrosum 15g.

Administration: Make a fine powder of the above ingredients. Take 9g once a day after mixing it with 30g of sugar and some boiling water.

1.5.2. Pillow for Clearing Head and Neck Ailment

Indications: Dizziness, tinnitus and stiff neck.

Prescription: Glycine Max 2500g, Flos Chrysanthemi Indici 500g, Herba Menthae (crystalized) 5g, Borneolum 3g.

Administration: Dissolve Herba Menthae and Borneolum in 500ml of water, put Glycine Max into the solution. When the water is absorbed, mix with Flos Chrysanthemi and then put it inside a pillow case. It is necessary to sleep on this pillow at least 8 hours for 3 nights before a satisfactory effect can be felt.

1.5.3. Decoction for Nourishing Blood

Indications: Dizziness due to deficiency of blood.

Prescription: Radix Angelicae Sinensis 24g, Rhizoma Ligustici 12g, Radix Rehmanniae Praeparata 30g, Semen Cassiae 3g, Herba Menthae 3g, Folium Nelumbinis 3g.

Administration: Make a decoction to be taken half in the morning, half in the evening.

1.6. Hysteria

1.6.1. Powder for Treating Hysteria

Indications: Unstable mood, timidness, suspicion, peculiar speech and insomnia.

Prescription: Radix Curcumae 100g, Alumen 60g, Semen Sinapis Albae 6g, Radix Glycyrrhizae Praeparata 2g, Cinnabaris 6g, Succinum 2g.

Administration: Grind the above ingredients into a fine powder. Take 3g twice a day with decoction of Pericarpium Citri Reticulatae 3g and Herba Menthae 3g.

1.6.2. Decoction of Fructus Tritici Levis

Indications: Depression, unstable mood, a feeling of foreign bodies in the throat.

Prescription: Radix Glycyrrhizae 12g, Concha Ostreae 18g, Fructus Tritici Levis 30g, Rhizoma Pinelliae 9g, Fructus Ziziphi Jujubae 12 Pcs.

Administration: Decoct the above ingredients twice and put the decoctions together. Take half of the volume in the morning, half in the evening.

1.6.3. Decoction of Nardostachyos and Pericarpium Citri Reticulatae

Indications: Dizziness, palpitation, insomnia, timidness, unstable mood, incoherent speech accompanied by general shivering and cramps in the limbs.

Prescription: Rhizoma Nardostachyos 30g, Pericarpium Citri Reticulatae 25g, Fructus Ulmi Pumilae(dried)15g.

Administration: Decoct the above ingredients twice and mix the decoctions together. Take half the volume in the morning, half in the evening. A treatment session consists of 10 days' medication.

1.7. Epilepsy and Mania

1.7.1. Heart-soothing Pill for Mania

Indications: Insanity, loss of consciousness, delirium, violence and failure to recognize people.

Prescription: Radix Euphorbiae Kansui 250g, Cinnabaris (Prepared with water)20g.

Administration: Soak Kansi in a clay pot for 1 hour, stew the pot with the fire by burning mulberry twigs for 1 hour and a half, then take out Kansi to dry. Afterwards grind Kansi into a powder after removing the cores. Mix the powder with the paste of Fructus Ziziphi Jujubae and make pills coated with Cinnabaris as big as mung beans. Take 1~2 pills with a decoction of peanut leaves(20g) once a day. Administrate with caution to the weak and old as well as pregnant women.

1.7.2. Medicated Soup of Owl and Lamb Heart

Indications: Epilepsy with a sudden fall and loss of consciousness, salivation, lockjaw, fixation of eyes and convulsions which occur irregularly.

Prescription: Owl 1, lamb heart 1 piece, Ramulus Uncariae 6g, Rhizoma Acori Graminei 6g.

Administration: Remove the internal organs of the owl and then put the lamb heart and the other two ingredients into the abdominal cavity and sew it up. After boiling it well, eat up the meat and soup in 2~3 days. Generally, after 3~5 sessions of treatment, the patient will be cured.

Note: Positive effects have been recorded in many cases.

1.7.3. Placenta Bolus

Indications: Epilepsy.

Prescription: Placenta of a donkey (baked brown and then ground into a powder) 1 piece, Rumulus Uncariae cum Uncis (powdered) 30g, Fungus Tremellae (powdered) 30g, crystal sugar (broken) 60g, vinegar 0.75kg.

Administration: First put Rumulus Uncariae cum Uncis and vinegar into a pot and decoct for 15 minutes, then take out the branches, pour the powder of Fungus Tremellae and crystal sugar into the decoction and boil for 10 minutes. Finally mix the decoction with the placenta and make boluses of 9g each. Take one bolus twice a day with plain water.

1.8. Insomnia

1.8.1. Sleeping Pill

Indications: Anxiety, sleeplessness and palpitation.

Prescription: Semen Ziziphi Spinosae (stir-fried) 30g, Poria 60g, Cinnabaris 10g.

Administration: Make a fine powder of Semen Ziziphi Spinosae and Poria, mix it with Jujube paste and make pills about the size of parasol seeds. And then coat the pills with Cinnabaris. Take 12 pills before sleep with plain water.

1.8.2. Egg Decoction for Insomnia

Indications: Insomnia, restlessness.

Prescription: Fructus Ulmi Pumilae (dried) 12g, Peanut leaves 30g, 1 egg (fresh).

Administration: Break the egg and stir it in a bowl. Make a decoction of about one bowl with Fructus Ulmi Pumilae and Peanut leaves. Then filter the decoction with gauze and pour the boiling decoction into the egg, continue to stir the decoction. Add some sugar and take the whole decoction before going to bed.

Note: This prescription can be applied to insomnia and restlessness caused by different diseases. While it treats insomnia and restlessness with remarkable result, it has no negative effect on patients who are using other medication at the same time.

1.9. Hypertension

1.9.1. Antihypertensive Bolus

Indications: Hypertension.

Prescription: Fructus Sophorae 500g, Herba Adianti 250g, Spica Prunellae 250g, Stigma Maydis 100g, Flos Chrysanthemi Indici 100g.

Administration: Make a fine powder of the above ingredients after drying them in the sun. Mix the powder with prepared honey and make boluses of 9g each. Take 1~2 boluses every morning and evening with water.

1.9.2. Antihypertensive Decoction

Indications: Hypertension.

Prescription: Ramulus Uncariae cum Uncis 30g, Ramulus Loranthi 30g, Lumbricus 10g, Concha Haliotidis 10g, Radix Achyranthis Bidentatae 12g, Flos Chrysanthemi Indici 9g, Radix Paeoniae Rubra 9g, Semen Ziziphi Spinosae 15g, Flos Carthami 3g, Radix Glycyrrhizae 3g, Rhizoma Acori Graminei 9g.

Administration: Decoct the above ingredients and take the

whole decoction once a day. Generally, an effective result can be felt after 6 doses.

1.9.3. Bolus for Treating Hypertension and Dizziness

Indications: Dizziness due to hypertension

Prescription: Goat horn 50g, Radix Scutellariae 6g, Radix Angelicae Sinensis 6g, Rhizoma Ligustici 6g, Radix Gentianae 6g, Cortex Moutan Radicis 6g, Rhizoma Gastrodiae 6g, Fructus Gardeniae (baked) 6g, Haematitum (crude) 6g, Ramulus Uncariae cum Uncis 6g, Periostracum Cicadae 6g, Ramulus Loranthi 6g, Lignum Dalbergiae Odoriferae 6g, Arisaema Cum Bile 6g, Rhizoma Pinelliae 6g, Radix Rehmanniae 10g, Spica Prunellae 10g, Cortex Eucommiae (baked) 10g, Concha Haliotidis 10g, Fluoritum 10g, Radix Paeoniae Alba 9g, Radix Bupleuri (prepared with vinegar) 9g, Folium Mori (frosted) 9g, Exocarpium Citri Grandis 9g, Radix Glycyrrhizae (powder) 9g, Plumula Nelumbinis 4g, Concha Cypraeae 15g, Radix et Rhizoma Rhei (prepared with wine) 12g, Borneolum Syntheticum 3g.

Administration: Make a fine powder of the above ingredients. Mix with processed honey and make boluses of 9g each, take 1 bolus twice a day with water.

1.9.4. Food of Six Red Ingredients for Lowering High Blood Pressure

Indications: Hypertension.

Prescription: Chinese sorghum 30g, Chinese kangduo (red) 30g, Semen Phaseoli 30g, Fructus Ziziph Jujubae 12Pcs, (Put the above 4 ingredients in a pot and cook). Peanut kernel (purplish red), soaked with vinegar for 7 days.

Administration: Take the meal for breakfast every morning with a suitable amount of peanut kernels. A treatment session consists of 7 days.

Note: An admirable effect has been achieved according to the clinical records of many patients. Usually, 4~5 sessions will lower the blood pressure to normal. The effect is also very stable.

1.10. Deviation of the Eye and Mouth

1.10.1. Honey Locust and Vinegar Lotion

Indications: Deviation of the eye and the mouth.

Prescription: Gleditsiae 7 Pcs, Spina Gleditsiae 6g, Mature Vinegar 200ml.

Administration: Pound Gleditsiae and Spina Gleditsiae and put them into a bottle; then pour vinegar into the bottle and soak for 7 days; afterwards, apply the liquid from Dicang point to Qianzheng point with absorbent cotton. Apply to the left side for right side deviation, to the right side for left deviation, 3~4 times a day. Avoid wind after the application.

Note: Never take it orally. A notable result can be achieved especially in mild cases and first time users. Usually. 4~5 days of treatment will bring about a cure.

1.10.2. Plaster for Correcting Deviation

Indications: Deviation of the eye and mouth

Prescription: Semen Papaveris 45 Pcs, Colophonium 15g, Resina Boswelliae Carteril 15g, Commiphora Myrrha 15g, Hydrargyrum 5g, Moschus 0.5g.

Administration: Make a paste of the above ingredients on a hard stone. Then spread the paste on a piece of cloth. Apply to the right side for left side deviation and apply to the left side for right side deviation. Avoid wind. Take off the plaster after recovery.

1.10.3. Cottonseed Bolus

Indications: Deviation of the eye and mouth.

Prescription: Cottonseed 50g, Resina Boswelliae Carteril 15g, Commiphora Myrrha 15g, Bombyx Batryticatus Praeparata 15g, Scorpio 12g, Rhizoma Typhonii Praeparata 12g, Rhizoma Gastrodiae 6g, Radix Glycyrrhizae 6g.

Administration: Make a fine powder of the above ingredients, mix with processed honey and make boluses of 6g each. Take 1 bolus twice a day with millet wine.

1.11. *Apoplexy*

1.11.1. Scolopendra Powder

Indications: Apoplexy manifested by paralysis or hemiplegia with aphsia.

Prescription: Scolopendra 10 Pcs, Gecko 10 Pcs.

Administration: Make a fine powder of the above ingredients after baking them brown on a tile. Take 1g each time, 2~3 times a day after mixing the powder with millet wine.

1.11.2. Bolus for Treating Apoplexy I

Indications: Apoplexy manifested by paralysis or hemiplegia, deviation of eyes or mouth and aphasia.

Prescription: Semen Strychni 500g, Atractylodis 45g, Herba Ephedrae 45g, Scorpio (tails) 45g, Bombyx Batryticatus 45g, Resina Boswelliae Carteril (prepared) 45g, Ancistrodon acutus 7 Pcs, Scolopendra 14 Pcs, Caulis Piperis Futokadsurae 60g, Radix Achyranthis Bidentatae 60g.

Administration: Soak Semen Strychni in urine of boys for 20 days, then soak in clean water for another 7 days and remove the peel. Dry it in shade, then scald it with sand until there is a popping sound. Make a fine powder of the other ingredients after baking them brown on a tile. Mix it with processed honey and make boluses of 3g each. Take 1 bolus twice a day with millet wine.

Note: Because of the large amount of Semen Strychni in the boluses, such phenomena as dry mouth and pain of the limbs may be found. Patients should drink plenty of water after taking the medicine.

Caution: Avoid tea, pork, mung beans and raw, cold, spicy food during the administration. Never administered to patients with hypertension.

In the case of a serious dry mouth and profuse prescription due to an overdose, a decoction of mung bean can mitigate the situation.

1.11.3. Bolus for Treating Apoplexy II

Indications: Hemiplegia complicated with deviation of eyes and mouth and aphasia.

Prescription: Flos Sophorae Immaturus 30g, Radix Angelicae Sinensis 10g, Rhizoma Ligustici 10g, Flos Carthami 10g, Scorpio 10g, Cortex Illicii 10g, Scolopendra 10g, Radix Aconiti 10g, Radix Cyathulae 10g, Ramulus Uncariae cum Uncis 10g, Bombyx Batryticatus 12g, Lumbricus 12g, Periostracum Cicadae 12g, Radix Ledebouriellae 9g, Radix Scrophulariae 9g, Poria 9g, Rhizoma Acori Graminei 9g, Arisaema Cum Bile 9g, Concretio Silicea Bambusae 9g, Caulis Piperis Futokadsurae 30g, Caulis Lonicerae 30g, Caulis Trachelospermi 30g, Radix Aristolochiae 30g, Caulis Millettiae Reliculatae 30g, Ramulus Loranthi 15g, Radix Morindae Officinalis 15g.

Administration: Make a fine powder of the above ingredients after drying them. Mix the powder with processed honey and make boluses of 6g each. Take 1 bolus 2~3 times per day with boiled water.

Note: A better effect will be achieved if the bolus is taken with the decoction of fresh parasol leaves (20g) or of fresh mulberry leaves (30g).

1.12. Numbness (*Appendix*: *Pain of the Waist and Leg*)

1.12.1. Egg Shell Powder

Indications: Numbness of limbs.

Prescription: Egg shell 100g, Semen Dolichoris Album 50g, Fructus Perillae 20g.

Administration: Make a fine powder of the above ingredients after baking them dry on a tile. Take 6g once a day with millet wine and water.

1.12.2. Wine Medicated with Scorpio and Fructus Chaenomelis

Indications: General numbness with soreness in loins and legs.

Prescription: Scorpio 40 Pcs, Fructus Chaenomelis 15g, Ramulus Cinnamomi 10g, Cortex Eucommiae 10g, Radix Cyathulae 10g, Flos Carthami 10g, Cortex Illicii 10g, Herba Ephedrae 6g, Caulis Piperis Futokadsurae 12g, Rhizoma Homalomenae 12g, Ramulus Loranthi 12g, white wine 1kg.

Administration: Soak the above ingredients in wine for 10 days. Take a small cup of wine (about 20ml) each time, twice a day. Add more wine if it is necessary. Never administered to pregnant women.

1.12.3. Tendon-relaxing Lotion

Indications: Numbness of limbs, arthralgia and general fatigue.

Prescription: Rhizoma seu Radix Noto-pterygii 10g, Radix Angelicae Pubescentis 10g, Resina Boswelliae Carteril 10g, Commiphora Myrrha 10g, Radix Glycyrrhizae 10g, Herba Lycopodii 10g, Atractylodis 10g, Rhizoma Atractylodis Macrocephalae 10g, Herba Schizonepetae 10g, Flos Carthami 10g, Caulis Piperis Futokadsurae 10g, Cortex Eucommiae (raw) 10g, Radix Aconiti Brachypodi 10g, Rhizoma Homalomenea 10g, Radix Aconiti Lateralis (raw) 10g, Radix Cyathulae 10g, Folium Artemisiae Argyi (raw) 10g, Lumbricus 10g, Pericarpium Citri Reticulatae 10g, Pericarpium Citri Reticulatae Viride 10g, Herba Incarvilleae Sinensis 15g, Rhizoma Gastrodiae 15g, Radix Ledeboariella 12g, Cortex Illicii 12g, Radix Arnebiae seu Lithospermi 6g, Radix Aconiti Kusnezoffii 6g, Squama Manitis 20g, Ramulus Loranthi 20g, Ramulus Cinnamomi 18g.

Administration: Decoct the above ingredients in an enamel basin. Fumigate the affected area for 30 minutes. Then, wash the affected area with the decoction once a day. One mixture can be used for 7 days.

1.12.4. Powder for Relieving Pain of the Waist and Legs

Indications: Pain in the waist and legs due to wind, cold and wetness.

Prescription: Squama Manitis (powder) 2g, pepper (powder) 70 Pcs, 4 eggs, sesame oil 100ml.

Administration: Boil the sesame oil in a pot. Beat the eggs in a bowl and mix it with the first two ingredients. Then, pour the mixture into the pot and fry it well. Eat up the fried eggs once, then wrap the affected area for the purpose of causing perspiration.

Note: Applications to many patients proved that 1~3 sessions of treatment will bring about a cure.

1.12.5. Decoction for Treating "Bi Syndrome"

Indications: Swelling and pain in the joints and limbs, dysbasia, numbness, limited movement due to the pain of the loins and joints.

Prescription: Radix Angelicae Sinensis 20g, Radix Astragali seu Hedysari 20g, Radix Achyranthis Bidentatae 20g, Ramulus Loranthi 20g, Radix Ledebouriellae 10g, Fructus Chaenomelis 10g, Fructus Gardeniae (baked) 10g, Radix Clematidis 10g, Radix Gentianae Macrophyllae 6g, Cortex Eucommiae 6g, Herba Lycopodii 6g, Radix Stephaniae Tetrandrae 6g.

Administration: Decoct the above ingredients. Take half the volume each time, twice a day.

1.12.6. Semen Strychni Pill

Indications: Pain of loins and legs due to cold and dampness, arthritis.

Prescription: Semen Strychni (prepared) 100g, Herba Ephedrae 30g, Resina Boswelliae Carteril (prepared) 30g, Commiphora Myrrha (prepared) 30g, Squama Manitis (prepared) 42g, Bombyx Batryticatus (baked) 42g.

Administration: Make a fine powder of the above ingredients. Mix it with millet gruel and make pills about the same size as mung beans. Adults take 6 pills before sleep to start with, then add one more pill each evening until the dosage reaches 20 pills. In cases of strong constitution, the number of pills may be increased to 30. In the case of pain in the loins and legs, take the pills with a decoction of Cortex Eucommiae (30g); In cases of arthritis, take the pills with a decoction of Radix Cyathulae (3g), Radix Stephaniae Tetrandrae (3g), Fructus Chaenomelis (3g).

Note: Avoid pork and mung beans during the administration. If there is profuse perspiration, dry mouth, cramp and dizziness, a decoction of mung bean will mitigate the situation.

1.13. Night Sweat
1.13.1. Sweat-stopping Decoction
Indications: Night sweat, cold sweat or spontaneous perspiration.

Prescription: Radix Allii Tuberosi 50g, Fructus Tritici Levis 50g, Fructus Ziziphi Jujubae 12 Pcs.

Administration: Decoct the above ingredients. Take both the decoction and Fructus Ziziphi Jujubae. Take the whole decoction once. Twice a day.

1.13.2. Powder for Treating Night Sweat
Indications: Night sweat due to deficiency of yin.

Prescription: Gecko 1.5g, Cinnabaris 0.3g, Semen Allii Tuberosi 0.5g.

Administration: Make a fine powder of the above ingredients. Mix the powder with cold water or saliva into a paste. Apply the paste on the navel covered with gauze, then fastened with adhesive plaster before going to bed. Romove it the next morning. 1~4 times will bring about a cure.

1.13.3. Decoction for Postpartum Sweating
Indications: Postpartum sweating.

Prescription: White sponge substance in the centre of corn stalks 15g, fine hairy roots grown in water of a willow tree 15g.

Administration: Decoct the above ingredients. Take the whole decoction once a day until perspiration ceases.

Note: This recipe has a quick effect on postpartum sweating. It is also effective in treating lack of lactation after childbirth.

1.14. *Stomachache*

1.14.1. Pill for Stomachache

Indications: Stomachache due to cold-evil.

Prescription: Rhizoma Alpiniae 60g, Rhizoma Zingiberis 45g, Rhizoma Nardostachyos 30g.

Administration: Make a fine powder of the above ingredients. Mix it with jujube paste and make pills as big as parasol seeds. Take 6 pills each time with brown sugar and water.

Note: This recipe can be used to stop stomachache due to cold food or cold attack in the night. One dose can achieve the effect. Never administered to patients with constipation or abdominal pain due to indigestion.

1.14.2. Powder of Os Sepiellae seu Sepiae and Peanuts

Indications: Gastric pain (e.g chronic gastritis), intermittent pain of long standing in the upper abdomen.

Prescription: Os Sepiellae seu Sepiae, Semen Arachidis Hypogaeae (raw), Semen Arachidis Hypogaeae (fried)

Administration: Prepare the same amount of the above three ingredients. Make a fine powder with them. Take doses of 12g three times a day before eating.

Note: Many patients have been cured after taking it for 1~3 months. Avoid alcohol and raw, cold, pungent food.

1.14.3. Powder of Three Burnt Ingredients

Indications: Gastric pain marked with distension in the chest, dyspepsia and belching.

Prescription: burned bun 100g, Fructus Crataegi (burned) 100g, Semen Arecae (carbonized) 12g, Radix Saussureae Lappae 12g, Fructus Amomi 12g, Fructus Alpiniae Galangae 18g, Endothelium Corneum Gigeriae Galli 24g, Holotrichia Diomphalia 20g.

Administration: Make a fine powder of the above ingredients. Take 4g each time with plain water, 3 times a day.

1.14.4. Powder of Cuttlebone and Evodia Fruit

Indications: Stomachache marked with heartburn and acid regurgitation.

Prescription: Os Sepiellae seu Sepiae (baked brown), Fructus Evodiae.

Administration: Prepare the same amount of the above ingredients, then make a fine powder with them. Take 3g 2~3 times with water each day.

Note: In the case of acid regurgitation and heartburn with no acid, take the decoction made of pepper (10 Pcs), Fructus Mume (3 Pcs), Fructus Ziziphi Jujube (5 Pcs), and eat the Fructus Ziziphi Jujube.

1.14.5. Powder for Relieving Three Pains

Indications: Gastric, abdominal and hernia pains.

Prescription: Fructus Meliae Toosendan, Semen Litchi, Fructus Foeniculi, Rhizoma Corydalis.

Administration: Prepare the same amount of the above ingredients and make a fine powder. Take 9g per time with water when you feel pain.

1.14.6. Stomach-soothing Powder

Indications: Epigastralgia, gastric or duodenal ulcer and chronic gastritis.

Prescription: A piece of tile (calcined) 100g, Pericarpium Citri Reticulatae 50g, Radix Paeoniae Alba 50g, Fructus Amomi 30g, Rhizoma Nardostachyos 30g, Radix Angelicae Sinensis 30g, Radix Astragali seu Hedysari 30g, Radix Glycyrrhizae 30g, Rhizoma Coptidis 10g, Radix Ophiopogonis 20g.

Administration: Make a fine powder of the above ingredients. keep it in a bottle to be used. Take 3g half an hour before eating, 3 times a day. 3 months can be a session.

Note: This recipe has a good effect in treating chronic gastritis. Avoid alcohol and any food which is cold, raw, pungent or sour.

1.15. Diarrhea (*Appendix*: *Dysentery*)

1.15.1. Powder for Stopping Diarrhea

Indications: Watery diarrhea, prolonged diarrhea.

Prescription: Galla Chinensis (baked brown) 30g, Rhizoma Atractylodis Macrocephalae (burned) 30g, Pericarpium Granati (baked) 20g, Semen Plantaginis (baked) 20g, Rhizoma Dioscoreae (raw) 20g, Alumen 15g.

Administration: Make a fine powder of the above ingredients. Take 6g 2~3 times a day with brown sugar and water.

1.15.2. Gruel of Rhizoma Dioscoreae for Stopping Diarrhea

Indications: Prolonged diarrhea and diarrhea before dawn due to deficiency of spleen.

Prescription: Rhizoma Dioscoreae (raw powder) 20g, Rhizoma Atractylodis Macrocephalae (burned) 4.5g, Poria 4.5g, Semen Plantaginis 4.5g, Semen Euryales 6g, Radix Astragali seu Hedysari (raw) 6g, Radix Gingseng 3g.

Administration: Put the above ingredients (except Dioscoreae) into water (500ml) and decoct for 30 minutes. Filter the dregs in the decoction and put Dioscoreae powder in it, then decoct them into gruel. Eat all of the gruel twice each day-morning and evening.

Note: Good effect can be achieved after one week of treatment.

1.15.3. Pill for Stopping Diarrhea and for Reinforcing Rectum

Indications: Long-standing diarrhea, prolapse of rectum.

Prescription: Halloysitum Rubrum 10g, Semen Myristicae 12g, Fructus Psoraleae 12g, husk of rice 6g.

Administration: Stew Myristicae and Fructus Psoraleae, then grind them together with the other two ingredients and make a fine powder to be used. Mix the powder with jujube paste and make pills about the same size as parasol seeds. Take 12 pills 3 times a day with millet gruel.

Note: In the case of prolonged prolapse of rectum, the dosage can be increased to 15~20 pills each time and taken preferably with a decoction of Radix Astragali seu Hedysari (15g) and Rhizoma Atractylodis Macrocephalae (12g).

1.15.4. Antidiarrheal Lotion

Indications: Diarrhea.

Prescription: Rhizoma seu Herba Saururi 60g, hust of sorghum 60g, Folium Ziziphi Jujubae 60g.

Administration: Decoct the above ingredients and wash the feet.

Note: Stop washing after diarrhea is relieved. Otherwise, a dry stool will result and this will render the treatment ineffective.

1.15.5. Pill for Arresting Dysentery

Indications: Dysentery, diarrhea.

Prescription: Radix Pulsatillae 300g, Radix Astragali seu Hedysari 300g, Radix Sophorae Flavescentis 300g, Radix Paeoniae Alba 150g, Radix Sanguisorbae 150g, Radix Glycyrrhizae 150g, Rhizoma Alismatis 100g, Caulis Akebiae 100g, Fructus Amomi 100g, husk of rice 50g, Semen Plantaginis 50g, Fructus Aurantii Immaturus 50g, Radix Aucklandiae 50g.

Administration: Make a decoction with Radix Sophorae Flavescentis and Glycyrrhizae. Make a fine powder of the other ingredients. Mix the decoction with the powder, make pills as big as mung beans, then dry them. Take 3~6g 2~3 times a day with water.

1.15.6. Powder for Treating Dysentery with Pus and Blood

Indications: Dysentery marked with fever, vomiting, purulent and bloody stool, abdominal pain with tenesmus.

Prescription: Rhizoma Coptidis 6g, Radix Saussureae Lappae 6g, Radix Scutellariae 6g, Semen Arecae 6g, Radix Paeoniae Alba 9g, Semen Coicis 12g, Pulvis Talci 10g, Radix Glycyrrhizae 3g.

Administration: Make a fine powder of the above ingredients. Children between 1~6 should take 0.3~1g per time; 6~12 years old should take 1~1.5g; above 12 years and adults should take 1.5~2g each time, 3 times a day after mixing it with sugar and water. Adjust the dosage according to the age and condition of the patient.

Note: Positive results have been found in thousands of cases.

1.15.7. Powder for Treating Bloody Dysentery

Indications: Dysentery with blood and pus in the stool.

Prescription: husk of rice 30g, Fructus Mume 24g, Herba

pteridis Multifidae 15g, Rhizoma Coptidis 12g.

Administration: Make a fine powder of the above ingredients. Take 2~3g each time, twice a day with sugar and water.

1.15.8. Bark and Peel Powder

Indications: Dysentery caused by prolonged diarrhea

Prescription: Jujube bark (baked brown) 100g, Cortex Ulmi Pumilae 100g, Pericarpium Granati (baked brown) 120g, Cortex Ailanthi 240g, Pericarpium Citri Reticulatae 50g.

Administration: Make a fine powder of the above ingredients. Take 6g 2~3 times a day with brown sugar and water.

1.15.9. Powder of Three Burnt Ingredients

Indications: Incessant dysentery with bloody stool.

Prescription: Radix et Rhizoma Rhei (carbonized), Fructus Mume (carbonized), Fructus Crataegi (carbonized).

Administration: Prepare the same amount of the above three ingredients and make a fine powder. Take 6g 2~3 times each day with millet gruel.

1.16. *Hepatitis* (*Appendix*: *Jaundice*)

1.16.1. Bolus for Treating Acute Icterohepatitis

Indications: Acute icterohepatitis.

Prescription: Radix Scutellariae 100g, Radix et Rhizoma Rhei 100g, Radix Gentianae 100g, Herba Plantaginis 50g, Radix Isatidis 50g, Herba Artemisiae Scopariae 50g.

Administration: Make a fine powder of the above ingredients. Mix with processed honey and make boluses of 6g each. Take 1 bolus twice each day with water.

1.16.2. Decoction for Soothing the Liver

Indications: Acute or chronis hepatitis.

Prescription: Radix Bupleuri 15g, Radix Curcumae 12g,

Radix Paeoniae Rubra 12g, Radix Gentianae 12g, Poria 12g, Fructus Gardeniae 10g, Semen Persicae 10g, Pericarpium Citri Reticulatae 10g, Carapax Trionycis (fried with vinegar) 14g, Rhizoma Dioscoreae (raw) 14g, Herba Artemisiae Scopariae 30g, Rhizoma Sparganii 6g, Radix Glycyrrhizae 6g.

Administration: Decoct the above ingredients. Take the whole decoction a day, half in the morning, half in the evening.

1.16.3. Jaundice-relieving Bolus

Indications: Jaundice.

Prescription: Ferrosi Sulfas 30g, Fructus Ziziphi Jujube 15g, Juglandis Regiae 40g, wheat seedling (frozen) q.s.

Administration: Deep fry the first 3 ingredients until they are burnt, then add wheat seedling and pound them into a paste. Make boluses of 3g each. Take 1 bolus every morning and evening with water.

Note: Avoid having pumpkin or meat.

1.16.4. Herba Artemisiae Scopariae Decoction for Treating Jaundice

Indications: Yang type jaundice (with yellow skin all over the body).

Prescription: Herba Artemisiae Scopariae 15g, Fructus Xanthii (baked) 15g, Pericarpium Citri Reticulatae 10g, Radix Paeoniae Alba 10g, Radix Bupleuri 6g, Radix et Rhizoma Rhei 6g, Rhizoma Coptidis 6g, Semen Pittospori 6g, Caulis Akebiae 4.5g, Herba Menthae 4.5g, Radix Trichosanthis 9g, Radix Saussureae Lappae 12g.

Administration: Decoct the above ingredients 3 times and mix the decoctions together. Take the whole decoction in one day, one third of the volume each time. Usually, 10 days of treatment will bring about a cure.

1.17. Constipation (Appendix: Bloody Stool)

1.17.1. Decoction for Moistening Intestines

Indications: Habitual constipation.

Prescription: Radix Angelicae Sinensis 12g, Semen Mori 12g, Semen Persicae (baked) 10g, Radix Ophiopogonis 10g, Radix Paeoniae Alba 24g, Radix Polygoni Multiflori 15g, Radix Glycyrrhizae (raw) 15g.

Administration: Decoct the above ingredients. Take one dose every day, half in the morning, half in the evening. Or grind the above ingredients into a powder and mix it with prepared honey in order to make boluses of 9g each. Take 1~2 boluses twice each day with water.

Note: According to clinical experience, 1~2 doses can bring about a cure. In serious cases, take boluses with the decoction.

1.17.2. Semifluid Extract for Moistening Intestines

Indications: Habitual constipation.

Prescription: Juglandis Regiae 250g, Semen Sesami 60g, Mel 200g.

Administration: Pound Juglandis Regiae and Semen Sesami into a paste. Mix it with Mel and store in a china pot to be taken 2 spoons every morning and evening with water.

Note: Avoid raw Chinese-onion and pungent food during treatment.

1.17.3. Bowel-relaxing Suppository

Indications: Serious constipation.

Prescription: Make a powder of Fructus Gleditsiae (peel and

seed removed) q. s., a spoonful of honey.

Administration: Boil the honey, then pour the powder into it and mix them into a soft dough. Rool the dough into a stick about 4cm. Insert the drug into the anus. There will be an immediate effect.

1.17.4. Cortex Ailanthi Bolus for Arresting Blood
Indications: Bloody stool.

Prescription: Cortex Ailanthi (baked brown) 100g, Corium Erinacei 150g, Flos Sophorae Immaturus (baked) 60g, Fructus Mume (burned) 24 Pcs.

Administration: Make a fine powder of the above ingredients, mix it with processed honey and make boluses of 9g each. Take 1 bolus every morning and evening with water on an empty stomach.

Note: This recipe is mainly used to treat fresh-bloody stool.

1.17.5. Decoction for Treating Bloody Stool
Indications: Prolonged fresh-bloody stool.

Prescription: Cortex Ailanthi (baked) 3g, Rhizoma Coptidis (baked) 3g, Radix Scutellariae (baked) 3g, Radix Sanguisorbae (burned) 6g, Fructus Mume 7 Pcs, Radix Paeoniae Alba (baked with wine) 12g, Colla Corii Asini 10g, Fructus Ziziphi Jujube 7 Pcs.

Administration: Decoct the above ingredients twice and put the decoctions together. Take the whole decoction in one day, half in the morning, half in the evening.

1.18. Dysuria

1.18.1. Decoction for Relieving Dysuria
Indications: Dysuria, distending pain in the lower abdomen.

Prescription: Fructus Kochiae 9g, Semen Plantaginis 9g Semen Malvae Verticillatae 9g, Fructus Gardeniae 6g, Semen Ailanthi 6g.

Administration: Decoct the above ingredients twice. Take the decoction in one day. Take one third of the volume each time.

1.18.2. Powder for Restoring Normal Urination

Indications: Dysuria.

Prescription: Alumen 30g, Sal 30g, Borneolum Syntheticum 0.5g, Moschus q. s.

Administration: Make a fine powder of the above ingredients. Divide the powder into 4 portions, pour one portion into the navel and drop cool water into it. The patient will urinate in half an hour.

Note: The ancient recipe had only 2 ingredients: Alumen and Sal. From clinical experience, we found a rapid effect can be achieved if Borneolum Syntheticum and Moschus are added.

1.18.3. Medulla Junci Decoction

Indications: Dysuria.

Prescription: Medulla Junci 6g, Semen Chrysanthemi Indici 6g, Semen Plantaginis 6g, Herba Lobeliae Radicantis 10g, Radix Ophiopogonis 12g.

Administration: Decoct the above ingredients. Take the whole decoction in one day, one third of the volume each time.

1.19. *Hiccup*

1.19.1. Decoction of Calyx Kaki

Indications: Hiccup.

Prescription: Calyx kaki 7 Pcs, Nodus Nelumbinis Rhizomatis 7 Pcs, Flos Syzygii Aromatici 12 Pcs.

Administration: Make a decoction of the above ingredients and take it only once.

1.19.2. Cigarette of Realgar and Nails

Indications: Obstinate hiccup.

Prescription: Realgar (powder) 0.5g, finger nails 2 Pcs.

Administration: Roll Realgar powder and the nails into a cigarette and smoke. The hiccup will stop at once.

1.19.3. Powder of Gallbladder and Semen Litchi

Indications: Hiccup.

Prescription: Pork gall-bladder 1 Pc, Semen Litchi 4 Pcs Fructus Aurantii 3g, Semen Phaseoli 10 Pcs.

Administration: Pound Litchi, Aurantii, Phaseoli into pieces and fill them into the gall-bladder. Dry the gall-bladder in shade, then make a fine powder. Take 1~1.5g twice a day with water.

1.19.4. Decoction for Treating Hiccup due to Qi Obstruction

Indications: Hiccup due to disorder of vital energy.

Prescription: Radix Codonopsis Pilosulae 15g, Pericarpium Citri Reticulatae 15g, Radix Linderae 12g, Ochra (boiled) 12g, Semen Arecae 10g, Lignum Aquilariae Resinatum (powder) 3g.

Administration: Decoct three times the above ingredients. excluding the last one which is infused with hot water and taken separately. Take the whole decoction in one day from time to time. Usually, 2~6 doses will bring about a cure.

1.20. *Vomiting*

1.20.1. Pill for Stopping Vomiting

Indications: Nausea, retch, vomiting after meals.

Prescription: Radix Glycyrrhizae (raw) 1000g, Terra Flava Usta 1000g, Radix Paeoniae Alba (raw) 500g, Pericarpium Citri Reticulatae 250g.

Administration: Make a fine powder of the first, third, fourth ingredients. Boil Terra Flava Usta in a basin and mix the powder with the clear liquid in the basin. Make pills about the size of mung beans and dry them in the shade. Take 6～9g 2～3times a day with water.

Note: A good effect can be achieved in treating gastric neurosis.

1.20.2. Powder for Treating Vomiting I

Indications: Sudden vomiting caused by different kinds of diseases.

Prescription: Lignum Aquilariae Resinatum 6g, Cortex Magnoliae Officinalis 12g, Pericarpium Citri Reticulatae 12g, Fructus Mume 12g, Caulis Bambusae in Taeniam 20g, Ochra 20g.

Administration: Make a fine powder of the above ingredients. Take the powder according to age and condition. Usually, 1～6g for babies, 9～12g for adults. Put the powder into a bowl and pour in boiling water (100～500ml), take it slowly when it is warm. The vomiting will stop.

1.20.3. Powder for Treating Vomiting II

Indications: Vomiting caused by asthenia or loose stool, nervous vomiting.

Prescription: Radix Ginseng 10g, Rhizoma Pinelliae 10g, Poria 10g, Caulis Bambusae in Taeniam 10g, Rhizoma Atractylodis Macrocephalae (burnt) 10g, Rhizoma Dioscoreae (raw) 40g, Halloysitum Rubrum 20g.

Administration: Make a fine powder of the above ingredients.

2~6g for babies, 10~12g for adults. While using, put the powder into a bowl or pot, infuse with boilng water (100~1000ml, according to the quantity of the powder); or decoct in a clay pot for 5~10 minutes and store in a thermos. Take the remedy from time to time.

Note: The above two recipes have proved to be effective after years of clinical practice. At the beginning of administration, a small dosage is recommended, which may increase gradually. In treating vomiting caused by other diseases, other drugs can be taken with the decoction till vomit stops.

1.20.4. Decoction for Treating Abdominal Pain and Vomiting

Indications: Stomachache, nausea, vomiting caused by deficiency and cold of the spleen and stomach.

Prescription: Radix Codonopsis Pilosulae 10g, Poria 10g, Fructus Evodiae 6g, Pericarpium Citri Reticulatae 6g, Rhizoma Zingiberis Recens 15g, Rhizoma Pinelliae 9g, Fructus Ziziphi Jujubae 5 Pcs.

Administration: Decoct the above ingredients twice and mix the decoctions well. Take the remedy from time to time. From clinical practice, most patients can fully recover after taking one dose.

1.20.5. Decoction for Arresting Vomiting

Indications: Morning sickness, vomiting of yellow fluid due to internal disorders or exogenous pathogenic factors in children.

Prescription: Rhizoma Coptidis 1.5g, Folium Perillae 2g, Caulis Ferillae 2g.

Administration: Make a decoction of the above ingredients. Take the whole decoction throughout the course of a day.

1.20.6. Ochra Powder

Indications: Vomiting after meal, vomiting due to functional disorder of stomach and intestines.

Prescription: Ochra 60g, Rhizoma Pinelliae Praeparatum 30g, Flos Syzugii Aromatici 15g, Radix Glycyrrhizae 15g, Borneolum Syntheticum 0.5g.

Administration: Make a fine powder of the first 4 ingredients, then add Borneolum Syntheticum and make a very fine powder. Store and seal the powder in a bottle. Adults take 3~4g 1~2 times a day with ginger decoction. For children, the dosage should be reduced with age.

1.21. Dysphagia

1.21.1. Bolus for Stopping Dysphagia and Globus Hystericus

Indications: Dysphagia, vomiting after meal, hiccup as well as globus hystericus.

Prescription: Radix Saussureae Lappae 9g, Fructus Perillae 9g, Borax 9g, Fructus Mume (without seeds) 12g, Fructus Amomi Rotundus 15g, Realgar 3g.

Administration: Make a fine powder of the above ingredients, then mix with processed honey and make boluses of 6g each. Take 1 bolus twice a day with water before eating. Patients with globus hystericus can put the bolus into their mouths in order to melt it. This achieves a better effect.

1.21.2. Powder of Baby Mice

Indications: Esophagus cancer, cardia cancer, vomiting after meal.

Prescription: Baby mice (newly-born, without hair) 10 Pcs, Realgar 1g.

Administration: Wrap the baby mice with dough, then put them into burning sawdust until the dough was burned dry. Remove the burned wrapper and make a fine powder together with Realgar. Divide the powder into 10 portions. Take 1 portion each day with water.

Note: This recipe was applied to patients with advanced esophagus cancer and advanced cardia cancer. These same patients were able to consume food after one or two doses.

1.21.3. Decoction for Dysphagia and Regurgitation

Indications: Dysphagia, regurgitation.

Prescription: Radix Codonopsis Pilosulae 20g, Rhizoma Dioscoreae (raw) 20g, Radix Paeoniae Alba (raw) 20g, Ochra 50g, Radix Asparagi 15g, Radix Angelicae Sinensis 15g, Caulis Bambusae in Taeniam 15g, Flos Carthami 3g, Semen Persicae (baked) 10g, Semen Impatientis 10g, Fructus Perillae (baked) 12g, Rhizoma Pinelliae 12g, reed root (fresh) 30g.

Administration: Decoct the above ingredients twice and mix them well. Take the whole decoction in one day, one third of the volume each time.

1.22. Pain in the Chest and Hypochondria

1.22.1. Qi-regulating Pill of Jujube

Indications: Pain, fullness and oppression in the chest.

Prescription: Blighted jujube 500g, walnut (broken, soaked in vinegar for 3 days, then carbonized) 500g, Nodus Nelumbinis Rhizomatis (dried) 250g.

Administration: Make a fine powder of the above ingredients. Mix with boiling vinegar and make pills as big as mung beans. Take 9~12g twice a day with water.

Note: This recipe is a folk prescription. It used to be a decoction for treating pain and fullness in chest and hypochondria caused by stagnation of vital energy. In clinical practice, pills can also achieve a good effect.

1.22.2. Juice of Fragrant-flowered Garlic

Indications: Stabbing pain in the chest.

Prescription: Fragrant-flowered garlic (fresh) 2500g.

Administration: Pound the garlic into a paste and get the juice. Take the juice from time to time.

Note: This recipe is from "Prescriptions for Emergency". In recent years, it proved effective in treating patients with chest pain (without organic pathological changes in heart and liver).

1.22.3. Decoction for Promoting Qi Circulation

Indications: Pain under hypochondria, depression of liver energy, oppression in the chest.

Prescription: Radix Codonopsis Pilosulae 10g, Rhizoma Pinelliae 10g, Radix Bupleuri 10g, Radix Rubiae 10g, Radix Paeoniae Alba 10g, Rhizoma Ligustici Chuanxiong 10g, Rhizoma Corydalis 10g, Pericarpium Citri Reticulatae Viride 10g, Fructus Aurantii 6g, Radix Scutellariae 6g, Radix Saussureae Lappae 6g, Radix Curcumae 6g, Radix Glycyrrhizae 6g, Rhizoma Cyperi 15g, Caulis Allii Fistulosi 3Pcs, Rhizoma Zingiberis Recens 3 Pcs.

Administration: Decoct the above ingredients twice and mix the decoctions well. Take the whole decoction in a day, half in the morning, half in the evening.

Note: Avoid anger, raw and cold food during the administration.

1.23. Stranguria

1.23.1. Pill for Relieving Five Kinds of Stranguria

Indications: Stranguria caused by urinary stone, disorder of vital energy; stranguria complicated by abdominal hematuria; stranguria complicated by chyluria; stranguria induced by overstrain.

Prescription: Talcum 150g, Gypsum Fibrosum 150g, Radix et Rhizoma Rhei 150g Radix Saussureae lappae 60g, Pericarpium Arecae 60g, Spora Lygodii 60g, Pericarpium Citri Reticulatae Viride 60g, Radix Paeoniae Rubra 60g, Succinum 60g, Radix Glycyrrhizae 30g, egg yolk (boiled with egg white removed) 12 Pcs.

Administration: Grind the above ingredients (except the egg yolks) into a fine powder. Mix the powder with the egg yolks and make pills as big as mung beans with the decoction of Herba Lophatheri, coated with Cinnabaris (fine powder, 100g), then dry them. Take 6g twice a day.

For stranguria caused by urinary stone, take the pills with the decoction of corn leaf 20g, corn root 20g and Caulis Akebiae 10g; for stranguria caused by disorder of vital energy, take the pills with the decoction of Fructus Foeniculi 12g and Pericarpium Citri Reticulatae 10g; for stranguria complicated by abdominal hematuria, take the pills with the decoction of Herba Seu Radix Cirsii Japonici 15g and Herba Cephalanoploris 15g; for stranguria complicated by chyluria, take the pills with the decoction of Radix Rehmannia 24g and Rehmanniae Praeparatae 24g; for stranguria induced by overstrain, take the pills with the decoction of Rhizoma Atractylodis Macrocephalae (burnt) 15g, Rhizoma

Dioscoreae (raw) 12g and Fructus Evodiae 9g.

Note: In clinical practice, you can adjust the dosage according to the patients' conditions.

1.23.2. Semifluid Extract for Treating Stranguria

Indications: long-standing stranguria with symptoms like a dull pain in lower abdomen and weakness.

Prescription: Radix Astragali seu Hedysari 500g, Herba Taraxaci (fresh) 1500g, Rhizoma Atractylodis Macrocephalae 250g, Rhizoma Dioscoreae (raw) 250g.

Administration: Put the above ingredients in a pot with suitable amount of water and decoct on a slow fire for 2 hours, then remove the residue and continue to decoct until it becomes a semifluid extract. Store it in a china bottle to be taken 1 spoonful of the semifluid extract 3 times a day with water.

Note: Avoid sexual intercourse during the administration.

1.24. *Diabetes*

1.24.1. Diabetes-relieving Bolus

Indications: Diabetes.

Prescription: Pork pancreas (baked dry) 7 Pcs, Fructus Schisandrae 100g, Radix Ophiopogonis 30g.

Administration: Make a fine powder of the above ingredients, mix it with prepared honey and make boluses of 9g each. Take 1 bolus twice a day with water.

1.24.2. Gruel of Rhizoma Dioscoreae and Cucurbita Moschata

Indications: Diabetes.

Prescription: The same amount of Rhizoma Dioscoreae (raw) and Cucurbita Moschata (dried).

Administration: Make a fine powder of the above ingredients. Make gruel with the powder (60~100g each time). Take once or twice a day.

Note: The ingredients can be replaced by fresh pumpkin and yam rhizome in summer and autumn when they are available, just cook and eat as food.

1.25. *Enuresis*

1.25.1. Powder of Rooster's Intestines

Indications: Enuresis, frequent micturition, bed-wetting in children.

Prescription: Rooster intestines (turned, cleaned and baked brown on a tile) 7 Pcs, boar bladder (baked brown on a tile) 7 Pcs, Fructus Schisandrae 20g, Fructus Rubi 30g.

Administration: Make a fine powder of the above ingredients. Fill the powder in Size 1 capsules. For adults, take 3 capsules 2~3 times each day; for children, take 1 capsule twice a day with water.

1.25.2. Decoction for Treating Enuresis

Indications: Fragility in the elderly, dizziness and soreness in the waist, weakness in the legs, enuresis due to kidney-deficiency.

Prescription: Radix Scutellariae 15g, Rehmanniae Praeparatae 15g, Radix Codonopsis Pilosulae 10g, Fructus Rubi 10g, Semen Cuscutae 6g, Fructus Schisandrae 6g, Semen Alpiniae Oxyphyllae 6g, Ootheca Mantidis 9g, Fructus Psoraleae 4.5g, Os Draconis 20g.

Administration: Decoct the above ingredients twice and mix the decoctions well. Take twice a day, half the volume in the morning, half in the evening.

Note: This recipe is also effective in treating children between 8~12 years old who suffer from enuresis due to weak constitution.

1.25.3. Decoction for Avoiding Bed-wetting

Indications: Bed-wetting in children.

Prescription: Pork bladder 1 piece, Semen Alpiniae Oxyphyllae 12 Pcs, Fructus Schisandrae 12 Pcs, Ootheca Mantidis 6 Pcs, Herba Ephedrae 3g.

Administration: Put the above ingredients into an earthenware pot and add some water. Then boil it (no salt). Eat the bladder as well as the soup. For children between 5~15 years of age, 1~3 times of treatment will stop enuresis.

1.26. Hernia

1.26.1. Powder for Treating Hernia

Indications: Hernia, swelling and bearing-down pain of unilateral testis.

Prescription: The same amount of Semen Litchi, Fructus Meliae Toosendan, Fructus Foeniculi, Fructus Evodiae and Radix Saussureae Lappae.

Administration: Soak the above ingredients in mature vinegar for a whole night, then take them out and bake brown on an old tile. Finally, grind the ingredients into a fine powder. Take 6~9g for adults, 2~3g for children, twice a day infused with water.

Note: This recipe used to be a decoction. The changed powder proved effective in clinical practice. In treating hernia and swelling & bearing-down pain of unilateral testis, 1~3 times of treatment can stop the pain. Most patients recover after a week of treatment.

1.26.2. Bolus for Treating Hernia
Indications: Hernia.

Prescription: Semen Citri Reticulatae 60 Pcs, Radix Angelicae Sinensis 100g, Retinervus Luffae Fructus 100g, Lignum Aquilariae Resinatum 30g.

Administration: Make a fine powder of the above ingredients after baking them on a tile until they are brown. Boil 300 Pcs of Chinese dates and remove the peel and seeds. Mix the dates with the powder and make boluses of 10g each. Take 1 bolus twice a day with a decoction of Fructus Foeniculi (6g).

1.26.3. Powder of Scolopendra
Indications: Hernia in children.

Prescription: Scolopendra 1 piece, 1 sparrow.

Administration: Prepare the sparrow (remove the internal organs and replace them with Scolopendra), then wrap the sparrow with touch paper then with mud (about 1cm thick). Put the sparrow near a fire, take off the mud after it is burnt. Make a fine powder of the sparrow. Take 3g three times a day. A reduced dosage for children under 5 years old.

1.27. *Nocturnal Emission*
1.27.1. Pill for Treating Nocturnal Emission
Indications: Nocturnal emission due to general debility.

Prescription: Endothelium Corneum Gigeriae Galli (scalded with sand) 20g, Galla Chinensis (soaked in salty water and baked brown) 30g, Corium Erinacei (baked brown on a tile) 45g, Ootheca Mantidis (baked to burnt) 60g

Administration: Make a fine powder of the above ingredients, sprinkle salty water and make pills about the same size as Semen Phaseoli. Dry the pills in the shade and coat them with Cinnabaris. Take 15~20 pills every evening before going to bed with salt water or plain water.

1.27.2. Powder for Stopping Nocturnal Emission

Indications: Seminal emission, spermatorrhea.

Prescription: Galla Chinensis (soaked in salty water for a whole night, baked brown) 3g, Os sepiellae seu Sepiae 3g, egg shell (soaked in salty water for a night, baked brown) 3g, Lithargyrum 3g.

Administration: Make a very fine powder of the above ingredients. Apply some vaseline to the glans penis then a little powder before sleep. The emission will stop.

1.27.3. Bolus of Sparrow Eggs and Semen Allri Tuberosi

Indications: Nocturnal emission, spermatorrhea.

Prescription: Semen Allii Tuberosi (baked) 18g, Ootheca Mantidis (carbonized) 45 Pcs, sparrow eggs 15 Pcs.

Administration: Grind the first 2 ingredients into a fine powder, then boil the eggs (remove the shell) and mix them with the powder. Sprinkle in some sugar and water and make 15 boluses. Take 5 boluses each night before sleep with plain water or salt water. Usually, 3 doses is sufficient for a positive result.

1.28. Impotence

1.28.1. Yang-restoring Powder

Indications: Impotence.

Prescription: Scolopendra (big) 20 Pcs, Herba Cynomorii 26g, Herba Epimedii 24g, Herba Cistanchis 30g, Radix Angelicae Sinensis 60g, Radix Paeoriae Alba 60g, Radix

Glycyrrhizae 60g.

Administration: Make a fine powder of the above ingredients. Take 4.5g twice a day with white wine.

1.28.2. Medicated Wine for Treating Impotence

Indications: Impotence.

Prescription: Fructus Lycii 50g, Cortex Cinnamomi (ground) 10g, white wine 500g.

Administration: Soak Fructus Lycii and Cortex Cinnamomi in the white wine for 7 days. Take 25~50ml every morning.

1.28.3. Snail Powder for Treating Impotence

Indications: Impotence.

Prescription: Cathaica Fasciola (shell, carbonized) 36 Pcs, Pork kidney 1 pair, Thea 3g.

Administration: Grind the Cathaica Fasciola shell into a fine powder, then divide it into 12 portions. Take 1 portion twice a day with the decoction of pork kidney and Thea.

1.28.4. Yang-reinforcing Decoction

Indications: Impotence.

Prescription: Fructus Lycii 6g, Semen Cuscutae 6g, Fructus Schisandrae 6g, Radix Aconiti Praeparata 6g, Herba Cynomorii 4.5g, Herba Epimedii 4.5g Herba Cistanchis 4.5g, Herba Dendrobii 4.5g, Fructus Psoraleae 4.5g, Radix Angelicae Sinensis 3g, Poria 3g.

Administration: Make a decoction of the above ingredients. Take half of the decoction in the morning, half in the evening.

1.29. Sterility Due to Deficiency of Sperms

1.29.1. Powder of Rehmanniae and Dioscoreae

Indications: Sterility due to deficiency of sperms.

Prescription: Rehmanniae Praeparatae (roasted dry) 300g, Rhizoma Dioscoreae 300g.

Administration: Make a fine powder of the above 2 ingredients. Infuse 30g powder with millet gruel (1 bowl). Take it every morning on an empty stomach. A persistent medication will bring about a cure.

1.29.2. Sperm-producing Bolus

Indications: Deficiency of sperms, dead sperms, impotence.

Prescription: Semen Cuscutae 60g, Fructus Psoraleae 60g, Herba Epimedii 60g, Herba Cistanchis 60g, Fructus Lycii 60g, Radix Rehmannia 60g, Rehmanniae Praeparatae 60g, Polygoin Multiflori Praeparatae 60g, Semen Allii Tuberosi (baked) 60g, Fructus Rosae Laevigatae 36g, Fructus Schisandrae 36g, Fructus Ligustri Lucidi 36g, Fructus Cnidii 36g, Radix Morindae Officinalis 42g, Placenta Hominis (powder) 60g.

Administration: Make a fine powder of the above ingredients, mix it with prepared honey and make boluses of 9g each. Take 1 bolus twice a day with water. A course lasts about one month. Usually, the patients will recover after 1~2 courses.

1.30. Constriction of Penis (Appendix: Priapism)

1.30.1. A Combined Recipe for Treating Constriction of Penis

Indications: Constriction of penis.

Prescription: Cauli Allii Fistulosi (15cm long) 1 stalk, old ginger (raw) 1 piece, white pepper 10g.

Administration: Grind the pepper to a fine powder and take the powder after mixing it with white wine. Then roast the ginger and insert it into the anus. Lastly, cut the two ends of the onion stalk, put one on the navel, press the other end with hot iron. The constriction of penis is cured.

1.30.2. Decoction for Relieving Priapism

Indications: Priapism.

Prescription: Retinervus Luffae Fructus (baked and powdered) 40g, Radix Scrophulariae 40g, Radix Ophiopogonis 40g, Cortex Cinnamomi 1 g.

Administration: Make a decoction of the last 3 ingredients. Infuse the powder of Retinervus Luffae Fructus twice with the decoction. Take half in the morning, half in the evening.

2. Surgery

2.1. Acute Mastitis

2.1.1. Paste for Relieving Acute Mastitis

Indications: Acute mastitis (not yet ulcerated) marked with swelling and distending pain.

Prescription: The same amount of Lumbricus (alive, cleansed) and Mirabilitum.

Administration: Pound the above two ingredients into a paste and mix well. Apply the paste to the affected area 2～3 times a day.

2.1.2. Mirabilitum Mixture

Indications: Mammary abscess and other abscesses not yet ulcerated.

Prescription: Cortex Phellodendri (powdered) 12g, Gypsum Fibrosum (powdered) 10g, Mirabilitum 10g.

Administration: Dissolve the Mirabilitum into water, then mix it with the other 2 ingredients into a paste. Apply the paste to the affected area twice a day.

2.1.3. Paste for Relieving Mammary Abscess

Indications: Mammary abscess (not yet ulcerated)

Prescription: Cactus 150g, Gleditsiae 5g, Radix et Rhizoma Rhei 10g.

Administration: Grind the second and third ingredients to a powder. Pound the Cactus and add in some vinegar, then pour in the powder and mix them into a paste. Apply the paste to the affected area once a day.

2.1.4. Fructus Trichosanthis Decoction

Indications: Swelling of the breast, early mammary abscess.

Prescription: Fructus Trichosanthis (not broken) 1 Piece.

Administration: Decoct the Fructus Trichosanthis for 1 hour and take the decoction. Afterwards pound the Fructus Trichosanthis and apply the paste to the affected area.

Note: The above 4 recipes prove to be effective in clinical practice. Most patients can recover after a short period of treatment.

2.1.5. Abscess-relieving Decoction

Indications: Early mammary abscess with symptoms like swelling and pain of the breast and galactostasis, in some cases it is complicated with fever and aversion to cold.

Prescription: Radix Angelicae Sinensis 10g, Cornu Cervi Degelatinatum 10g, Squama Manitis 10g, Fructus Trichosanthis 10g, Radix Trichosanthis 10g, Fructus Forsythiae 9g, Bulbus Fritillariae Thunbergii 9g, Flos Lonicerae 20g, Herba Taraxaci 15g, Herba Violae 15g, Resina Olibani Praeparata 6g, Myrrha Praeparata 6g.

Administration: Decoct the above ingredients twice and put the decoctions together. Take half in the morning, half in the evening.

Note: In the case of hard swelling without ulcer, put more water to make the decoction. Take the decoction and at the same time, apply the hot residue to the affected area, which helps stop the swelling and pain.

2.2. Pyogenic Infection and Ulcerous Disease of Skin

2.2.1. Powder for Relieving Ulcerous Disease of Skin

Indications: Pyogenic infection, furuncle, carbuncle on the nape, carbuncle around the shoulder blade and other unnamed swelling poison as well as scrofula.

Prescription: Hydrargyrum 6g, Colophonium 6g, Camphora 5g, Minium 5g, Borneolum Syntheticum 5g, Aerugo 3g, Camphora 9g.

Administration: Make a fine powder of the above ingredients, store it in a china bottle to be used. Then melt one antitoxic plaster, put 1g the above powder in the centre of the plaster and mix them well. Apply it to the affected area after the powder is soaked into the plaster.

Note: This recipe can be used in treating early pyogenic infection, pustule and ulcer of different stages. It is successful in relieving swelling and pain, Promoting tissue regeneration and healing the affected area.

2.2.2. Five-twig Ointment for Restoring Yang

Indications: Pyogenic infection and carbuncle of different kinds

Prescription: Peach twigs, twigs of Chinese scholartree, willow twigs, twigs of mulberry tree, elm twigs. (prepare 12 pieces of each kind of twigs, 4cm long each) hair 12g, cèra Flava 30g, sesame oil 200ml.

Administration: Put the above 5 kinds of twigs and the hair in a pot, pour into it the sesame oil and soak for a night. Fry them on a small fire till the twigs dry up. then filter the dregs. Add Cèra Flava to the oil, and mix them into an ointment after Cera Flava is dissolved and cooled. Store the ointment in a porcelain jar. Now Wash and sterilize the affected area, then apply to it a plaster made of the ointment and a piece of gauze. Change the medicine every other day.

2.2.3. Ointment for Treating Carbuncles Around the Shoulder Blade

Indications: Carbuncles around the shoulder blader with rotten tissue.

Prescription: Indigo Naturalis 6g, Fuligo E Herbis 9g, Caulis Allii Fistulosi 7 Pcs, Semen pruni Armeniacae (with peel and tip removed) 7 Pcs, Calomelas 0.5g, Borneolum Syntheticum 0.5g, honey 1 cup.

Administration: First pound Caulis Allii Fistulosi and Semen pruni Armeniacae on a piece of limestone, then add the rest ingredients and pound them into a paste. Put the paste evenly on a piece of cloth and apply to the affected area. Remove the plaster 7 days later, by then the festered tissue will come off.

Note: A slight pain may be felt at the beginning of medication, and there will be constant pus discharging from the affected area, just clean the pus and do not remove the plaster till after 7 days.

2.2.4. Paste for Malignant Lentigo

Indications: Malignant lentigo (no suppuration).

Prescription: Resina Olibani 1.5g, Myrrha 1.5g, Resina Draconis 1.5g, Fructus Mume 0.3g, egg white q.s.

Administration: Grind the first 4 ingredients and then add a little egg white to make an ointment. Apply the ointment to the affected part and cover it with a bamboo leaf.

Note: This prescription can relieve pain and swelling in cases of various furuncles at the beginning stage with severe pain.

2.3. Pustule of the Finger Tip

2.3.1. Pustule-curing Egg

Indications: Pustule of the finger tip.

Prescription: One fresh egg, Alumen (powdered) 1.5g.

Administration: First break a small hole on the egg shell, stir the white and yolk with a chopstick, then add Alumen powder into the egg and mix them well. Insert the affected finger inside the egg, securing the egg with paper sealed around, 1~2 times of treatment will bring about a cure.

2.3.2 Pustule-curing Ointment

Indications: Pustule of the finger tip.

Prescription: Alumen (powdered) 3g, Herba pteridis Multidae q.s. Fructus Mume (pounded) 7 Pcs.

Administration: First pound Herba pteridis Multidae in a bowl, then add the other ingredients and pound them into a paste. Apply the paste to the affected area twice a day.

2.4. Furuncle (Appendix: Inflammatory Disease With Redness of Skin)

2.4.1. Ointment for Treating Furuncle

Indications: Furuncle.

Precription: Caulis Allii Fistulosi 3 inches long, honey 1 cup, Alumen (powdered) 10g.

Administration: Pound Caulis Allii Fistulosi, then add honey and Alumen powder and mix them well. Apply the ointment to the affected area twice a day, covered and secured with a dressing.

Note: This is a much used prescription, clinical experience proves its effectiveness.

2.4.2. Anti-toxic Decoction
Indications: Unbearable painful swell due to furuncle
Prescription: Flos Lonicerae 30g, Radix Trichosanthis 30g, Radix et Rhizoma Rhei 20g, Prepared Resira Olibani 15g, Prepared Myrrha 15g, Squama Manitis 10g, Herba Violae 10g, Spina Gleditsiae 9g, Scolopendra 1 piece.
Administration: Decoct twice the above ingredients and put the decoctions together. Take half of the decoction in the morning, half in the evening.

2.4.3. Five-twig Ointment
Indications: Serious cases of furuncle
Prescription: 5 kinds of twigs from peach, willow, elm, Chinese scholartree and white mulberry, 60g each, Resina Olibani 15g, Myrrha 15g, Minium 50g, sesame oil 250g.
Administration: First cut the twigs into 2cm long and fry them in sesame oil till they dry up. Remove the twigs from the oil and put Resina Olibani (powdered) and Myrrha (Powdered) into the oil and stew them into a semi-fluid, then slowly add Minium and mix them well. The ointment is ready when cooled. Apply some ointment on the affected area once a day.
Note: The ointment functions well in relieving pain and swelling and also in promoting the growing of new tissue.
Generally, after it is applied, the pain will stop instantly.

2.4.4. Chrysanthemum Decoction
Indications: The onset of furuncle.
Prescription: the whole plant of chrysanthemum (including root, stem and leaves) 40g, Herba Violae 30g, Radix Angelicae Sinensis 36g, Radix Glycyrrhizae 12g.
Administration: Make a decoction with the above ingredients,

one dose a day, half in the morning, half in the evening.

2.4.5. Yellow Powder
Indications: Inflammatory disease with reddness of skin, burning sensation and continuous itching as well as pain.

Prescription: Radix et Rhizoma 30g, Rhizoma Coptidis 10g, Cortex Phellodendri 20g, Realgar 6g.

Administration: Make a powder of the above ingredients, mix them well with 2g of Borneolum and some vinegar to be applied to the affected area.

2.4.6 Decoction of Periostracum Cicadae and Two Kinds of Flowers
Indications: Inflammatory disease with reddness of skin.

Prescription: Periostracum Cicadae 10g, Flos Lonicerae 20g, Chrysanthemum 15g, Herba Taraxaci 30g, Herba Violae 30g.

Administration: Make a decoction with the above ingredients. Take the whole decoction a day.

2.5. Carbuncle on the Back or on the Nape
2.5.1. Powder for Romoving Rotten Tissue
Indications: Carbuncle on the back or nape with rotten tissue.

Prescription: White pepper 50g, Fructus Mume 5g.

Administration: First make a powder of the white pepper, then add Fructus Mume for further grinding till it becomes a fine powder. Store the powder in a porcelain bottle. Apply a tiny portion to the rotten tissue after routine cleaning of the affected part, 1~2 times each day.

Note: The powder can only be used in removing rotten tissue and it is ineffective to common carbuncles.

2.5.2. Powder of Resina Olibani and Radix et Rhizoma Rhei (Appendix: Bile and Ink Paste)

Indications: Carbuncle on the back, migrant erysipelas.

Prescription: Resina Olibani 5g, Radix et Rhizoma Rhei 20g, Semen Sojae Praeparatum 20g, red-skinned garlic 1 bulb.

Administration: Pound the above ingredients into a paste and apply it to the affected area, then spread Folium Artemisiae Argyi on the place and light fire to burn the leaves.

Appendix: Bile and Ink Paste. Rub an ink stick against an inkstone with bile and mature vinegar, then apply the paste to the affected area frequently to keep the place wet.

2.5.3. Carbuncle-curing Lotion

Indications: Carbuncle on the back, carbuncle on the nape as well as multiple furuncles.

Prescription: Periostracum Serpentis 5g, Scorpio 10 Pcs, Scolopendra 3 Pcs, vinegar 150ml.

Administration: Put the first 3 ingredients into the vinegar and soak for 7 days. Apply the liquid many times a day to the affected area with a piece of obsorbent cotton.

Caution: Not to be in contact with mouth, nose or eyes.

2.6. Scrofula

2.6.1. Scrofula-treating Lotion of Spiders

Indications: Scrofula.

Prescription: Big spiders 60 Pcs, Purple-skinned garlic 6 bulbs.

Administration: Spiders caught in mid-summer are put into a glass bottle, squeeze the garlic juice out and put the juice into the same bottle. Seal the bottle with wax and bury the bottle 40cm deep in the sunny place. Unearth the bottle the following summer, open the bottle in order to allow for the toxic gas to come out. Then filter the liguid with a gauze. Before it is applied, the affected part should be washed with salty water and then dried , then use a piece of absorbent cotton to smear over the area with the medicated liquid. Use once every other day for over a month.

2.6.2. Scolopendra Powder

Indications: Scrofula with ulcer and unhealing sore.

Prescription: Golden-headed Scolopendra 2 Pcs, Cortex Lycii Radicis 6g, Galla Chinensis (the whole) 1 Piece.

Administration: First drill a small hall on the gall of Calla Chinensis and dump out the inside things and fill it with the powdered Scolopendra and Cortex Lycii Radicis. Then wrap 10 layers of touch paper (wet with water) around the gall and scald it with wheat bran in a pan. Stir the wheat bran and the wrapped gall till 10 layers of paper are all burnt (After the wheat bran has turned black, it should be replaced). Then remove the burnt paper and grind the gall into a fine powder, add a little Mochus. Grind again and mix them well. When used, the powder (the quantity of which is decided by the area of affection) is mixed with vinegar and put on a piece of oily paper. Apply the paper to the affected part once a day.

2.6.3. Suppositories Made of Donkey-hide Gelatin

Indications: Scrofula with lingering ulcers.

Prescription: Donkey-hide gelatin made in Donge, Shandong province.

Administration: Soften the gelatin with warmth and make suppositories of various sizes and coin-like slices. Wash the affected part and choose the appropriate suppository to be put on or inserted into the ulcerated area. Change the suppositories once every 2~3 days. Clinical practice with hundreds of patients proved that a satisfactory result can be achieved within a short period of time, either in the case of scrofula or carbuncles.

2.7. *Small Boils Near the Hairline*

2.7.1 Earthen Vat Powder
Indications: Small boils at the back of one's neck near the hairline.

Prescription: Broken old earthen vat one piece (about 5g), Alumen 10g.

Administration: Calcine the earthen piece till it is red, pour vinegar onto it and it breaks. Grind the broken pieces with Alumen into a fine powder, and then add sesame oil to make a paste. Apply the paste to the affected part twice a day.

2.7.2. Three Ashes Plaster
Indications: Small boils at the back of one's neck near the hairline.

Prescription: Nidus Vespae (carbonized) 15g, frost-beaten muberry leaves (carbonized) 15g, hair (carbonized) 10g, Galla Chinensis 6g, Calomelas 2g, Borneolum, 1g.

Administration: Grind the above ingredients into a fine powder and mix it with processed honey. Make plasters with the mixture and apply them once a day to the affected places.

2.7.3. Herba Equiseti Hiemalis Plaster
Indications: Small boils at the back of one's neck near the hairline.

Prescription: Herba Equiseti Hiemalis 30g, Semen Phaseoli 30g, Flos Sophorae Immaturus 25g, Alumen 15g.

Administration: Make a fine powder of the above ingredients. Boil some sesame oil for 15 minutes then turn off the fire. Put the powder into the oil when it is warm, mix them into an ointment. Put a little ointment onto a piece of cloth and then apply it to the affected part. The plaster is to be changed once every 3 days.

2.8. *Pustulosis Bullous*

2.8.1. **Realgar Powder**

Indications: Carbuncles manifested by yellowish discharge, itching and lingering ulcer which is off and on.

Prescription: Realgar 6g, Cortex Phellodendri 6g, Alumen 6g.

Administration: Grind the above ingredients into a fine powder and mix it with the bile of a pig's gallbladder, then apply the paste to the affected part after washing it with warm water.

2.8.2. **Powder of Exocarpium Citrulli**

Indications: Pustulosis bullous.

Prescription: Exocarpium Citrulli (carbonized) q.s. Borneolum (powdered) a little.

Administration: Grind them into a powder and spread it on the affected part; or mix the powder with sesame oil and smear the ointment on the affect part.

2.8.3. **Powder of Indigo Naturalis and Cortex Phellodendri**

Indications: Pustulosis bullous.

Prescription: Indigo Naturalis and Cortex phellodendri of equal quantity.

Administration: Grind the two ingredients into a fine powder and mix it with sesame oil. Apply the paste to the affected place 1~2 times a day.

2.9. Ecthyma

2.9.1. Ecthyma Plaster

Indications: Long-standing and intractable ecthyma.

Prescription: Clean pig hair 10g, Squama Manitis 6g, Resina Olibani 6g, Myrrha 6g, Galla Chinensis 6g, Beeswax (to be added late) 30g, sesame oil 200ml.

Administration: Put the above ingredients into a pan to be soaked in the oil for one night. Then fry them on a small fire till they dry up, remove the dregs, boil again till a drop poured out will form a ball. Now add beeswax and mix them well. When it is cooled down, the ointment is ready for use. Store the ointment in a porcelain utensil. For application, make a plaster with some of the ointment and a piece of gauze which is then applied to the sterilized affected area. Change the gauze once a day or once every other day.

2.9.2. Hair Powder

Indications: Ecthyma.

Prescription: Human hair and pig's hair of equal amount (carbonized together).

Administration: Grind the ashes into a powder, mix it with sesame oil and apply the paste to the affected place once a day or once every other day.

2.9.3. Convenient Ointment

Indications: Ecthyma, pustulosis bullous, scabies as well as intractable ulcerated sores.

Prescription: Nidus Vespae (high up on a building preferable) 1 Piece (about 10g), Colophonium 20g, sesame oil 50ml.

Administration: Break the nest and fry it in sesame oil, when the nest dries up, add and melt Colophonium. Then remove the pan off the fire and grind the cooled substance into a fine powder. Now heat 150ml of sesame oil in a pan till a drop poured out from it forms a ball, then turn off the fire and cool the oil a little, afterwards add the powder little by little while stirring the oil. When cooled down, the ointment is ready and can be put into a porcelain container. For application, take a little out to be spread on the affected area after a clean-washing of the place, then cover it with a piece of gauze. Change the gauze once a day or once every two days.

2.10 Scrofula Around the Neck

2.10.1 Powder of Realgar and Gecko

Indications: Scrofula around the neck with severe pain.

Prescription: Realgar and Gecko of equal amount.

Administration: Grind the two ingredients into a fine powder and mix it with some sesame oil. Apply the paste to the affected place and the pain will be alleviated. Generally, $3 \sim 4$ times of application will bring about a cure.

2.10.2 Calx Powder (Appendix: Herba Erodiiseu Geranii)

Indications: Scrofula around the neck.

Prescription: Calx 1 Piece.

Administration: Prepare Calx with water, then dry it in a ventilated place. Afterwards grind it into a powder and mix the powder with sesame oil to make a paste. Apply the paste $2 \sim 3$ times a day to the affected area.

Appendix: Herba Erodiiseu Geranii (fresh) q. s. is collected in summer and pounded into a paste which is applied $1 \sim 2$ times a day to the affected place. Generally, $2 \sim 3$ days' treatment will bring about a cure.

2.11. Scaby Head

2.11.1. Powder for Scaby Head

Indications: Scaby head.

Prescription: Big black wasps' nest 1 Piece, Alumen powder, Colophonium powder and Minium powder all of equal amount.

Administration: Fill the holes of the nest with the three powders. Then melt it on fire and stir-fry it till it dries up. Finally, grind it into a powder and mix the powder with sesame oil. Apply the paste once a day to the affected place.

2.11.2 Ointment for White Ringworm

Indications: White ringworm.

Prescription: Aerugo 10g, Folium Artemisiae Argyi 10g, Folium Sophorae (tender twigs) 20g, human hair 5g, sesame oil 250ml, Cera Flava (to be added late) 50g.

Administration: Soak the above ingredients (excluding Cera Flava) in sesame oil for 2 days in a porcelain basin. Then fry the ingredients till they dry up, remove the dregs and reheat the medicated oil till a drop poured out will form a ball. Stop the fire and add Cera Flava into it and mix them into an ointment. Wash the affected part before applying the ointment to it once a day.

Note: Meat and spicy food should be avoided during medication.

2.12. Alopecia Areata

2.12.1. Powder for Alopecia Areata

Indications: Alopecia areata.

Prescription: Sulfur 12g, Realgar 12g, Lithargyrum 12g,

Membrana Follicularis Ovi 12g, Radix Sophorae Flavescentis 12g, Calomelas 6g.

Administration: Grind the above ingredients into a fine powder which is applied to the affected area twice a day by dipping fresh ginger slices in the powder.

2.12.2. Hair-growing Bolus

Indications: Alopecia areata, trichomadesis.

Prescription: Fructus Mori 12g, Fructus Rosae Laevigatae 20g, Semen Cuscutae 12g, Galla 10g, Fructus Lycii 18g, Flos Chrysanthemi 24g, Semen Juglandis 18g, Glycine Max 20g, Radix Polygoni Multiflori 12g, Rehmanniae Praeparatae 20g, Radix Angelicae Sinensis 12g, Rhizoma Ligustici Chuanxiong 6g, Cortex Moutan Radicis 6g, Herba Schizonepetae 6g.

Administration: Mix the above ingredients together and grind them into a fine powder. Make boluses of 9g each with the powder and processed honey. Take 1 bolus twice a day with plain water.

Note: While taking the bolus, rub the affected place with prickles of young gourds. Generally, new hair will grow after half a month's administration.

2.12.3. Semen Strychni Oil

Indications: Alopecia areata.

Prescription: Semen Strychni 3 Pcs, sesame oil 50ml.

Administration: Fry Semen Strychni in the oil till it becomes burnt and black, then remove it and store the oil in a bottle. Prick the affected area with a needle to get a slight bleeding, then spread the oil onto the area with a feather. The oil should be applied for no more than once a day.

2.13. Scabies

2.13.1. Tadpole Drink

Indications: Scabies.

Prescription: Live tadpoles (medium size preferable) 15 ~ 20g.

Administration: Collect tadpoles with a net during spring or summer when they are plenty in the pond and river, wash them with cooled boiled water, add some vinegar and take the whole drink once a day for 4~6 days.

Note: Dried tadpoles can substitate for live ones. Grind the dried tadpoles into a powder which can be taken 3~6g once a day with half boiled water and half vinegar.

2.13.2. Sulfur Lotion

Indications: Pyoderma.

Prescription: Sulfur 100g, Calx 200g.

Administration: Put the above two ingredients and 1000ml of water into an earthenware pot to be decocted until 500ml of decoction is left. Wash the affected area with the cleared portion of decoction 2 ~ 3 times a day. Generally, one week's washing will bring about a cure.

2.13.3 Folium Typhonii Lotion

Indications: Scabies with severe itch.

Prescription: Folium Typhonii q. s.

Administration: Make a decoction with the leaves and wash the affected area with it 1~2 times a day. Generally, the itch stops after second wash and a week's wash may bring about a cure.

Caution: The decoction should not be taken orally, as it is poisonous.

2.14. Tinea (Appendix: Goose Foot Tinea)

2.14.1. Natrii Sulfas Ointment

Indications: Intractable chronic eczema with unbearable itch.

Prescription: Natrii Sulfas, Rhizoma Dryopteris, Radix Euphorbiae Ebracteolatae, Semen Persicae (unprepared) all of equal amount.

Administration: Mix the above ingredients and grind them into a powder, then make an ointment by mixing the powder with vaseline. Before application, wash the affected part and scrape off the dead skin with a knife. Then spread the ointment over the place once a day.

2.14.2. Alumen Powder

Indications: Psoriasis.

Prescription: Alumen, white poplar bark, peach tree bark, Radix Allii Tuberosi all of equal amount.

Administration: Grind the above ingredients into a powder which is mixed with sesame oil, apply the paste to the affected part once a day.

Note: Wash and scrape off the dead skin before medication.

2.14.3. Ointment for Tinea

Indications: Tinea

Prescription: Cacumen Biotae (fresh) 250g, vinegar 1000g.

Administration: Soak the leaves in the vinegar for one night, then decoct it till half volume is left. Remove the leaves, heat again till it becomes a semi-fluid. Wash the affected area and then apply the medicine to the area, covering it with a dressing. Change the medicine and dressing once a day.

Note: Incision therapy can be applied to reinforce the treatment effect.

2.14.4. Hank-soaking Lotion (Appendix: Semen Strychni Oil)

Indications: Goose-foot tinea, dryness, itch, pain and skin-shedding of the palms.

Prescription: Radix Aconiti, Radix Aconiti Kusnezoffii, Rhizoma Acori Graminei, Fructus Gleditsiae Abnormalis, Bombyx Batryticatus, Herba Spirodelae, Herba Incarvilleae Sinensis, Cortex Dictamni Radicis, Squama Manitis, Radix Clematidis, Cortex Lycii Radicis, Radix Ledebouriellae, Lumbricus and Radix Angelicae Pubescentis 10g each, mature vinegar 1000g.

Administration: Soak the above ingredients in the vinegar for 2 days, then decoct for half an hour, remove off the fire. Keep the hands in the lukewarm decoction for 15~20 minutes 2~3 times a day. The lotion may be used for 7 days.

Appendix: Semen Strychni Oil. Semen Strychni (10 Pcs) are fried in 50ml of sesame oil till they dry up. Remove the seeds and apply the oil to the affected part.

2.15. Intertrigo Eczema Behind the Ear

2.15.1. Powder for Ear Eczema (Appendix: Cortex Phellodendri Powder)

Indications: Intertrigo eczema behind the ear.

Prescription: Squama Manitis 6g, Minium (stir-fried) 4.5g, lead powder (stir-fried) 4.5g, Calomelas 0.5g.

Administration: Grind the above ingredients into a fine powder and mix the powder with sesame oil. Apply the paste to the affected part 1~2 times a day.

Appendix: Cortex Phellodendri Powder. Grind some amount of Cortex Phellodendri into a fine powder and mix it with sesame oil. Apply the paste to the affected place 1~2 times a day.

2.16. Fire Burn and Scald

2.16.1. Ointment for Fire Burn and Scald (Appendix: Recipe I, II)

Indications: Fire burn, scald.
Prescription: Galls on the willow leaves.
Administration: Collect the galls in early summer, remove the foreign substances inside the galls, bake them in a pan till they are half burnt. Then grind them into a fine powder and mix it with sesame oil. Put the ointment in a sealed earthenware utensil and steam it for 1 hour. Now clean affected area, cut open the blisters to get rid of the liquid inside before applying a thin layer of the ointment to the affected area. No dressing is needed. The ointment is used 1~2 times a day.
Note: The recipe is good at clearing away heat and toxin, antiinfection as well as moistening the dryness and promoting the growing of new tissues. Clinical practice proves its quickness in relieving pain. No scar is left after healing.
Appendix: Recipe I. Melt 60g of alkali in a bowl, apply the liquid with absorbent cotton 2~3 times a day to the affected area.
Recipe II. Mix sesame oil with honey (both of same amount) and apply the mixture to the affected place. White sugar can be substituted for honey if honey is not available.

2.17. Vitiligo

2.17.1. Powder for Vitiligo

Indications: Vitiligo

Prescription: Sulfur 9g, Realgar 12g, Lithargyrum 6g, Calomelas 6g.

Administration: Grind the above ingredients into a fine powder. Apply the powder with an end of a cucumbar to the affected area. If a cucumbar is not available, mix the powder with vinegar and apply the paste to it.

2.17.2. Mylabris Lotion

Indications: Vitiligo.

Prescription: Mylabris 6 Pcs, Huechys Sanguinea 6 Pcs, Alumen 6g.

Administration: Soak the above ingredients in 150ml of vinegar for 24 hours after pounding them. Apply the clear lotion with absorbent cotton to the affected skin. Stop application when the skin blisters. Do not take the lotion orally as it is highly poisonous.

2.18. Acne

2.18.1. Decoction for Acne

Indications: Acne.

Prescription: Herba Schizonepetae 12g, Radix Ledebouriellae 9g, Radix Platycodi 9g, Rhizoma Ligustici Chuanxiong 6g, Fructus Aurantii Immaturus 9g, Fructus Forsythiae 9g, Fructus Gardeniae 9g, Radix Angelicae Sinensis 9g, Rhizoma Coptidis 6g, Radix Scutellariae 6g, Radix Glycyrrhizae 6g, Radix Angelicae Dahuricae 4.5g, Herba Menthae (to be added late) 3g.

Administration: Decoct the above ingredients. Take half of the decoction in the morning, half in the evening after heating it. 6 doses make up a treatment session. During administration, hot and spicy, much seasoned food as well as toilet soup and facial cream should be avoided.

2.18.2. Acne Cream

Indications: Acne.

Prescription: Calomelas, Pollen powder of Typhonii, Radix Scutellariae, Radix Angelicae Dahuricae all of equal amount, honey q. s.

Administration: Grind the above ingredients into a fine powder, mix it with honey to make a cream. Apply a bit (like a soybean in size) to the face while washing the face in the morning and evening. Wash the cream off after 1~2 minutes.

Note: The cream is not to enter the eyes or mouth, as it is highly poisonous. During medication, toilet soap, facial cream, fat, alcohol and spicy food should be avoided.

2.19. *Paronychia*

2.19.1. Rhizoma Rhei Powder

Indications: Paronychia.

Prescription: Rhizoma Rhei 10g, mole crickets (baked dry) 2 Pcs.

Administration: Grind the two ingredients into a fine powder and then mix it with vinegar. Apply the paste to the affected part once a day.

Note: Clinical application shows that the above recipe cures paronychia with fast effect.

2.19.2. Pollen Powder of Typhonii

Indications: Paronychia.

Prescription: Pollen from Typhonii (collected in blossom).

Administration: Grind the pollen and spread the powder on the affected place.

Note: When pollen is not available, roots (Rhizoma Typhonii) may be used as a substitute. First cut the peeled roots into slices, then grind them into a powder and mix it with white wine. Apply the paste to the affected area and cover the place with a dressing. Generally 3 ~ 4 times of medication will bring about a cure.

2.20. *Tetanus*

2.20.1. Powder for Treating Tetanus

Indications: Tetanus.

Prescription: Goat horn 24g, rooster's dung (baked yellow on a tile) 24g.

Administration: Mix and grind the two ingredients into a fine powder. Take 6g each time after mixing it with millet wine. Stay in a warm bed in order to promote perspiration.

2.20.2. Decoction of Periostracum Cicadae

Indications: Tetanus.

Prescription: Periostracum Cicadae (head and feet removed) 15g, Ramulus Indigoferae (fresh 100g, or dry 60g).

Administration: Make a decoction of the above ingredients. Take the whole decoction a day for the light case, and 2 decoctions for the severe one. Children take half the dose.

2.20.3. Decoction for Expelling the Wind Evil

Indications: Tetanus, convulsions of the four extremities and lockjaw.

Prescription: Periostracum Cicadae 30g, Scolopendra 1 Piece,

Scorpio 7 Pcs, Bombyx Batryticatus 7 Pcs, Ramulus uncariae cum Uncis 10g, Rhizoma Gastrodiae 10g, Rhizoma Arisaematis 6g, Cinnabaris (powdered, to be taken separately with water) 1.5g.

Administration: Make a decoction of the above ingredients (excluding Cinnabaris), add a little wine to the decoction and take it once every 4 hours.

2.21.　Corn

2.21.1.　Corn-removing Paste

Indications: Corns on toes.

Prescription: Flos Carthami 30g, Cortex Lycii Radicis 60g.

Administration: Grind the above ingredients into a fine powder and make a paste with the powder and sesame oil. Then wash the affected part with warm water, cut off the outer skin and apply the paste to it, cover the area with a dressing. Reapply the paste once every 2 days. Generally, the corn falls off after 3~4 times of application.

2.21.2.　Powder of Calx and Alkaline

Indications: Corn.

Prescription: Calx, alkaline of equal amount.

Administration: Grind the two ingredients into a fine powder and mix the powder with water. Apply the paste to the affected place once every 2 days. Generally the corn falls off after 2~3 applications.

2.22.　Wart

2.22.1.　Lotion of Kelp and Rhizoma Cyperi

Indications: Wart on face and body.

Prescription: Fresh kelp root 200g, fresh Rhizoma Cyperi

150g.

Administration: Cut the 2 ingredients into little bits and store them in a bottle, add 100 ml of water. The lotion is ready after 7 days. Apply the lotion 3~4 times a day to the affected area and in 1~2 weeks, the wart will disappear.

Note: Pull the wart and bind it with a thread of a spider's web (about 20cm long) around the bottom. As the cobweb contracts, the wart will fall off in 3~4 days.

2.23. Itch and Swell of Scrotum
2.23.1. Wash Lotion for Scrotum Ailment

Indications: Pain and swell of scrotum, complicated by skin-shedding and unbearable itch.

Prescription: Fructus Kochiae 30g, Herba Spirodelae 30g, Calyx Fici Caricae (double amount if fresh) 30g.

Administration: Put the ingredients into an enamel basin, add some water, and heat it until it boils, Fumigate and wash the affected part once a day.

2.24. Chilblain
2.24.1. Powder of Freshwater Mussel Shell

Indications: Chilblain with ulcer.

Prescription: Freshwater mussel shell 100g, Os Draconis 50g.

Administration: Calcine the two ingredients and then grind them into a powder. Apply the powder to the affected area. For severe cases, apply the paste made by mixing the powder with sesame oil to the affected area once a day. 2~3 applications will bring about a cure.

2.25. Appendicitis

2.25.1. Decoction for Treating Appendicitis

Indications: Appendicitis.

Prescription: Radix Angelicae Sinensis 9g, Rhizoma Cyperi Praeparata 9g, Radix et Rhizoma Rhei 9g, Radix Platycodi 9g, Fructus Meliae Toosendan 9g, Radix Saussureae Lappae 9g, Fructus Forsythiae 9g, Radix Rehmanniae 12g, Cortex Moutan Radicis 12g, Flos Lonicerae 20g, Herba Taraxaci 20g, Semen Persicae (stir-fried, skin and tips removed) 10g, Radix Scrophulariae 6g, Resina Olibani Praeparata 6g, Myrrha Praeparata 6g, Radix Glycyrrhizae 6g, Caulis Spatholobi 15g, Semen Benincasae 30g.

Administration: Decoct the above ingredients and take half of the decoction in the morning, half in the evening.

Note: The dregs of the decoction are wrapped in a piece of cloth as a hot compress in order to heat the affected place while the dregs are hot. Hot salt (1 000g) may also be wrapped as a hot compress which can be applied many times a day.

3. Gynecology

3.1. *Amenorrhea*

3.1.1. Decoction of Radix Angelicae Sinensis

Indications: Amenorrhea.

Prescription: Radix Sinensis 15g, Radix Salviae Miltiorrhizae 15g, Radix Rubiae 10g, Radix Achyranthis Bidentatae 9g, Flos Carthami 9g.

Administration: Decoct the ingredients twice, add brown sugar 50g and a cup of baby's urine into the decoction. Take half the volume in the morning, half in the evening. Generally, 2~3 days' treatment will bring about a cure.

3.1.2. Pill of Three Yellow Ingredients for Restoring Menstruation

Indications: Amenorrhea in virgin complicated with abdominal pain and distension.

Prescription: Rhizoma Curcumae Longae (sliced) 150g, Radix et Rhizoma Rhei (prepared with vinegar) 150g, Radix et Rhizoma Rhei (fresh) 150g.

Administration: Grind the above ingredients into a very fine powder. Boil some vinegar and mix the powder with the boiling vinegar. Make pills as big as mung beans and dry them for use. Take 6g of pills 3 times a day with water and brown sugar. 4 days is the length of a treatment session.

Note: During medication, millet, mung beans as well as raw,

cold and spicy food should be avoided.

3.1.3. Pill for Treating Amenorrhea

Indications: Blood exhaustion in women leading to amenorrhea.

Prescription: Radix Angelicae Sinensis 30g, dried undergrown dates 30g, Flos Carthami 45g, Radix Ginseng 6g, Semen Persicae (stir-fried, with skin and tips removed) 24g.

Administration: Mix the ingredients and grind them into a fine powder. Make pills as big as Chinese parasol tree seeds with date paste and the powder, coated by Cinnabaris. Take 10 ~15 pills twice a day with much splashed water.

3.2. Dysmenorrhea

3.2.1. Decoction for Relieving Pain During Menstruation

Indications: Severe abdominal pain and distension during menstruation.

Prescription: Pollen Typhae 6g, Faeces Trogopterorum 6g, Radix Paeoniae Rubra 6g, Rhizoma Ligustici Chuanxiong 6g, Radix Salviae Miltiorrhizae 9g, Radix Linderae 9g, Rhizoma Cyperi (prepared with vinegar) 12g, Resina Olibani Praeparata 3g, Myrrha Praeparata 3g, Rhizoma Corydalis 4.5g.

Administration: Decoct twice the above ingredients and put the decoctions together. Take half the volume in the morning, half in the evening.

Note: This recipe is to be used 3 days before menstruation. With 3 months' administration, the pain and distension will vanish.

3.2.2. Herba Leonuri Pill

Indications: Painful menstruation.

Prescription: Herba Leonuri (stir-fried) 24g, Fructus Crataegi (carbonized) 20g, Rhizoma Cyperi (prepared with vinegar) 20g, Pollen Typhae (prepared and fresh) 10g respectively, Faeces Trogopterorum (stir-fried) 9g, Rhizoma Corydalis 4.5g.

Administration: Grind the above ingredients into a very fine powder, make pills with water (with size like mung beans) and dry them for use. Take 3g 3 times daily with the decoction of fresh ginger and brown sugar.

3.2.3. Decoction for Expelling Cold Invasion Prior to Menstruation

Indications: Cold invasion prior to menstruation resulting in painful menstruation.

Prescription: Folium Artemisiae Argyi (stale) 10g, Rhizoma Cyperi 10g, Rhizoma Alpiniae Officinarum 12g, brown sugar 40g.

Administration: Decoct the first 3 ingredients and pour the hot decoction into the brown sugar to be taken once.

Note: Clinical experience shows that dysmenorrhea caused by wind-cold invasion, raw and cold food or exposure to rain is generally cured with one dose.

3.3. *Retrograde Menstruation*

3.3.1. Decoction for Retrograde Menstruation

Indications: Retrograde menstruation (perverse flow of menses, bleeding from mouth and nose)

Prescription: Rhizoma Ligustici Chuanxiong 6g, Rhizoma Rehmanniae Praeparatae 15g, Radix Angelicae Sinensis 10g, Rhizoma Atractylodis Macrocephalae (carbonized) 10g, Poria 10g, Radix Astragali seu Hedysari 10g, Radix

Paeoniae Alba 10g, Herba Leonuri 10g, Radix Notoginseng (Powdered and taken seperately with water) 1g.

Administration: Decoct twice and mix the decoctions together. Take half amount in the morning and half in the evening.

Note: For long-standing retrograde menstruation, the decoction may be taken 3~5 days prior to menstruation, generally, 3~5 days' administration may bring about a cure.

3.3.2. Powder for Perverse Flow of Menses

Indications: Retrograde menstruation with massive bleeding from mouth and nose complicated by dizziness and palpitation and, in severe cases, loss of consciousness.

Prescription: Donkey-hide gelatin 30g, Folium Artemisiae Argyi (stale, stir-fried) 30g, Crinis Carbonisatus 30g, Os Draconis 15g, Pollen Typhae (carbonized) 15g, Radix Rehmanniae (fresh, baked dry) 36g, Cinnabaris 12g, Radix Notoginseng (powdered) 6g.

Administration: Mix and grind the above ingredients into a very fine powder. Take 9~12g 2~3 times a day with decoction of joints of lotus roots.

3.3.3. Os Draconis Powder for stopping Bleeding (Appendix: Decoction of Four Fresh Ingredients)

Indications: Bleeding from nose resulted from perverse flow of menses or other causes.

Prescription: Gypsum Fibrosum 6g, Concha Ostreae 6g, Os Draconis 6g, Crinis Carbonisatus 3g.

Administration: Grind the above ingredients into a very fine powder and blow a tiny portion of it into a bleeding nostril with a rolled paper, the bleeding will stop instantly.

Appendix: Decoction of Four Fresh Ingredients Fresh joints of lotus roots 20 pcs, fresh chives 60g, fresh Cacumen Biotae

60g, Fresh baby urine half a cup, millet wine 100ml. Decoct the ingredients and take 1/3 of the decoction in the morning, 1/3 at noon, and 1/3 in the evening.

3.4. Uterine Bleeding

3.4.1. Decoction for Treating Uterine Bleeding by Strengthening Qi

Indications: Incessant uterine bleeding leading to prostration of qi due to miscarriage in woman.

Prescription: Radix Astragali seu Hedysari (prepared) 24g, Radix Angelicae Sinensis (washed with wine) 12g, Radix Paeoniae Alba (stir-fried with wine) 12g, Rhizoma Astractylodis Macrocephalae (carbonized) 12g, Radix Ginseng (decocted separately and taken together) 12g, Cortex Eucommiae (carbonized) 6g, Radix Polygalae 6g, Fructus Schisandrae 6g, Radix Rehmanniae Praeparata 15g, Arillus Longan 15g, donkey-hide gelatin (melted) 20g, Radix Glycyrrhizae (powdered) 3g.

Administration: Decoct the above ingredients. Take the decoction frequently in severe cases or twice a day in minor ones. The decoction should last one day in both cases.

3.4.2. Powder for Consolidating Blood

Indications: Uterine bleeding.

Prescription: Corium Erinacei (baked brown) 1 sheet, palm bark (carbonized) 45g, Pollen Typhae (carbonized) 45g, silkworm cocoons (half-burnt) 100 Pcs, Crinis Carbonisatus 24g.

Administration: Grind the above ingredients into a fine powder. Take 6g twice a day with warm millet wine.

3.4.3. Powder of Three Carbonized Ingredients

Indications: Uterine hemorrhage.

Prescription: Retinervus Luffae Fructus (carbonized), palm bark (carbonized) and Folium Artemisiae Argyi (carbonized) three of equal amount.

Administration: Grind them into a fine powder. Take 12～20g each time with warm millet wine.

3.4.4. Powder of Herba Cephalanoploris

Indications: Metrorrhagia, hematemesis and epistaxis.

Prescription: Herba Celphalanoploris (lumps on the stem, collected in summer and autumn, dried) q. s.

Administration: Stir-fry the drug in an earthenware pan till it becomes burnt. Grind it into a powder and take 3～6g 2～3 times a day with water.

3.5. Leucorrhagia

3.5.1. Decoction for Treating Leucorrhagia

Indications: Abnormal vagina discharge.

Prescription: Radix Codonopsis Pilosulae 12g, Rhizoma Dioscoreae 12g, Semen Coicis 12g, Cortex Phellodendri (salted) 6g, Semen Ginkgo (stir-fried) 6g, Cortex Moutan Radicis 6g, Rhizoma Alismatis 6g, Pericarpium Citri Reticulatae 6g, Radix Rehmanniae Praeparata 30g, Rhizoma Atractylodis 10g, Semen Plantaginis (stir-fried with wine) 10g, Radix Glycyrrhizae 3g, Fructus Ziziphi Jujubae 12 Pcs.

Administration: Make a decoction of the above ingredients. Take half the decoction in the morning, half in the evening when it is warm. In cases of yellowish leucorrhea, add Poria 10g, Semen Euryales (stir-fried) 30g to the above recipe; in cases of reddish leucorrhea, add Concha Ostreae (calcined) 3g, Flos Sophorae Immaturus (stir-fried) 3g and grind them into a powder which is taken after mixing it with water.

3.5.2. Powder for Treating Leucorrhagia
Indications: Profuse and incessant vagina discharge.
Prescription: Os Sepiellae seu Sepiae 20g, Radix Angelicae Dahuricae 20g, Fructus Foeniculi (stir-fried) 20g, Concha Ostreae 32g, Cortex Phellodendri (salted) 12g, Pericarpium Citri Reticulatae 12g, Semen Plantaginis (stir-fried with wine) 40g, Radix Paeoniae Alba (stir-fried) 30g.
Administration: Grind the above ingredients into a fine powder, and take 6g twice a day with water.
Note: Pills can also be made with the powder and water.

3.5.3. Egg of Semen Ginkgo and Fructus Piperis Nigri
Indications: Leucorrhagia
Prescription: One fresh egg, Semen Ginkgo (powdered) 3 Pcs, Fructus Piperis Nigri (powdered) 7 Pcs.
Administration: Break a small hole on the egg shell, put the two powders inside, seal the egg and boil it in a half wine and half vinegar liquid. Eat the well-boiled egg and the illness will pass.

3.6. *Morning Sickness*
3.6.1. Fructus Mume Decoction
Indications: Morning sickness.
Prescription: Fructus Mume 7 Pcs, Pericarpium Citri Reticulatae 6g, Fructus Amomi 6g, Lignum Aquilariae Resinatum 4.5g, Rhizoma Pinelliae 4.5g, Caulis Bambusae in Taeniam 9g, Rhizoma Dioscoreae 9g, Rhizoma Atractylodis Macrocephalae (carbonized) 9g, Radix Glycyrrhizae 3g,

fresh ginger 3 slices.

Administration: Decoct the above ingredients. Take the decoction every now and then till vomiting stops.

3.6.2. Drink of Terra Flava Usta

Indications: Morning sickness.

Prescription: Terra Flava Usta 12g, Halitum 3g, Calyx Kaki (powdered) 6g.

Administration: Put the above ingredients in a bowl and pour boiling water into the bowl while stirring quickly to have it well-mixed. Take frequently when the liquid is clear.

3.7. Fetus-soothing

3.7.1. Fetus-soothing Decoction

Indications: Threatened abortion manifested by a bearing down sensation in the lower abdomen and abdominal pain.

Prescription: Radix Angelicae Sinensis 10g, Fructus Psoraleae 10g, Cornu Cervi gelatin (melted) 10g, Rhizoma Atractylodis Macrocephalae (carbonized) 15g, Radix Rehmanniae Praeparatae 15g, Cortex Eucommiae (stir-fried) 6g, Radix Dipsaci 6g, Radix Paeoniae Alba 12g, Ramulus Loranthi 9g, Folium Artemisiae Argyi (stir-fried) 3g, Semen Cuscutae 4.5g.

Administration: Make a decoction of the above ingredients. Take one dose a day for 3 days prior to the time when the last abortion took place. Then take one dose every 10 days until 6 months' pregnancy. Afterwards 20 days a dose till one month before delivery.

Note: Hundreds of pregnant women with a history of habitual abortion all successfully avoided abortion and had a full-term delivery after taking the decoction.

3.7.2. Powder for Treating Threatened Abortion
Indications: Threatened abortion.

Prescription: Semen Dolichoris Album (stir-fried slightly) 4.5g, Calyx Cucurbita Moschata (baked brown on a tile) 10g, Colla Cornus Cervi 10g.

Administration: Grind the first two ingredients into a fine powder, add Colla Cornus Cervi, and pour boiling water to it. Take the liquid one dose per day for the severe cases and one dose every other day for the light ones.

3.8. Frequent Urination During Pregnancy (Appendix: Dysuria)
3.8.1. Folium Kochiae Decoction
Indications: Frequent and scanty urination with continuous dripping during pregnancy.

Prescription: Folium Kochiae 100~150g.

Administration: Make a decoction to be taken by mouth.

Appendix: Dysuria. Pericarpium Zanthoxyli 10g, Halitum 10g. Grind them into a powder, mix the powder with proper amount of Caulis Allii Fistulosi and pound them into a paste. Apply the paste to the navel and donot remove the paste till urination returns to normal.

3.9. Postpartum Abdominal Pain
3.9.1. Powder for Relieving Abdominal Pain
Indications: Postpartum abdominal pain.

Prescription: Radix Angelicae Sinensis 9g, Resina Olibani Praeparatae 6g, Faeces Trogopterorum 3g, Pollen Typhae 3g.

Administration: Grind the above ingredients into a fine powder. Take 6g twice a day with a decoction of Fructus Crataegi (30g).

3.9.2. Decoction for Warming the Meridians to Relieve Pain

Indications: Severe abdominal pain caused by wind-cold attack to the lower abdomen after delivery.

Prescription: Radix Angelicae Sinensis 12g, Rhizoma Ligustici Chuanxiong 9g, Rhizoma Atractylodis Macrocephalae 9g, Rhizoma Corydalis 9g, Radix Codonopsis Pilosulae 10g, Rhizoma Zingiberis 3g, Fructus Evodiae 6g, Cortex Cinnamomi 6g, Ramulus Cinnamomi 6g, Radix Glycyrrhizae (prepared) 6g.

Administration: Make a decoction of the above ingredients. Take half the decoction in the morning and half in the evening.

3.10. *Postpartum Faintness*

3.10.1. Quick-acting Powder for Postpartum Faintness (**Appendix**)

Indications: Postpartum faintness.

Prescription: Radix Angelicae Sinensis (stir-fried) 4.5g, Herba Schizonepetae (carbonized) 3g, Herba Artemisiae Anomalae (carbonized) 3g.

Administration: Grind the above ingredients into a powder. Heat half a cup of baby's urine and proper amount of wine, pour the hot liquid into the powder and take all the mixture.

Appendix: Mature vinegar 1 bowl, limestone 1 piece. First bake the stone on fire till it is red, then soak the red stone into the bowl of vinegar, the steam of which will make the patient regain consciousness. This recipe is effective in treating postpartum faintness due to loss of profuse blood after delivery.

3.10.2. Drink of Cinnabaris and Baby's Urine

Indications: Loss of consciousness after delivery.

Prescription: Cinnabaris (prepared with water), baby's urine q. s.

Administration: Put Cinnabaris in a bowl, find a healthy child (below 5 years of age) to urinate into it. Mix the Cinnabaris with urine and give it to the patient.

3.11. Promoting Lactation (Appendix: Lactifuge)

3.11.1. Pig's Trotter Soup for Promoting Lactation

Indications: No milk production after delivery.

Prescription: A pair of sow's trotters, Radix Angelicae Sinensis 9g, Radix Angelicae Dahuricae 9g, Fructus Liquidambaris 9g, Cornu Cervi Degelatinatum 9g, Squama Mantis 9g, Radix Rhapontici seu Echinopsis 9g, Semen Vaccariae (popped) 9g, Rhizoma Ligustici Chuanxiong 6g, Medulla Tetrapanacis 6g, Radix Astragali seu Hedysari 12g.

Administration: Stew the trotters first and decoct the other ingredients with trotter soup. Take half the soup in the morning and half in the evening.

3.11.2. Powder of Squama Manitis and Colla Cornus Cervis (Appendix: Recipe I, II)

Indications: Lack of milk, insufficient milk production.

Prescription: Squama Manitis, Colla Cornus Cervis, Semen Vaccariae (stir-fried) all of equal amount.

Administration: Grind them into a fine powder. Take 6g of the powder twice a day with either hen soup or pig's trotter soup.

Appendix: Recipe Ⅰ: To prevent lack of milk, the affected woman may drink brown sugar and hot water with 7～8 drops of blood from the cut-off umbilical cord. Recipe Ⅱ: For those with no milk secretion after delivery, drink a bowl of willow roots (grown in water, 30g) decoction all at once, and try to sweat a little. Generally 2～3 doses can bring about a cure.

3.11.3. Malt Decoction for Lactifuge

Indications: Stuffiness of breasts after stopping breast feeding.

Prescription: Fructus Hordei Germinatus (stir-fried) 90g, medicated leaven (stir-fried) 40g, Herba Taraxaci 40g.

Administration: Make a decoction to be taken half in the morning and half in the evening. Generally 2～3 doses will bring about a cure.

3.12. *Pruritus Vulvae*

3.12.1. Five Leaves Washing Lotion

Indications: Pruritus vulvae (trichomonas vaginitis).

Prescription: Leaves of peach tree 100g, of fig tree 100g, of moxa 100g, of lotus 100g, of summer cypress 100g.

Administration: Put all the leaves into an enamal basin, add water and boil 15 minutes. Fumigate and wash the affected place. 2～3 times of administration (in light cases) will bring about a cure; for the severe ones, 4～5 times will do.

4. Paediatrics

4.1. Infantile Malnutrition

4.1.1. Powder for Treating Infantile Malnutrition

Indications: Emaciation, sallow complexion, pot-belly, sparce and dry hair in children who cry easily and constantly suck their fingers.

Prescription: Endothelium Corneum (scalded with sand) 30g, Squama Manitis 30g, Carapax Trionycis (prepared) 30g, Semen Arecae (stir-fried) 30g, Rhizoma Atractylodis Macrocephalae (carbonized) 24g, Semen Torreyae 20g, Fructus Crataegi (carbonized) 12g, Fructus Hordei Germinatus (carbonized) 12g, Massa Fermentata Medicinalis 12g, Fructus Amomi 9g, apricot leaves 3g.

Administration: Grind the above ingredients into a very fine powder. Take the powder 3 times a day with sugar and water. Children between 6 months and 1 year take 0.2~0.3g each time, 1~3 years 0.3~0.6g, 3~6 years 0.6~1g, 6~12 years 1~1.5g each time.

4.1.2. Nutrition-improving Powder

Indications: Infantile malnutrition with abdominal distension and anorexia.

Prescription: Rhizoma Rhei 30g, Semen Arecae (carbonized) 30g, Semen Pharbitidis 15g, Pericarpium Citri Reticulatae 24g, Radix Glycyrrhizae 12g.

Administration: Grind the above ingredients into a powder. Children between 6 months and 12 years may take from 0.2g to 0.6g accordingly before breakfast with sugar and water.

Caution: The powder should not be administered to children who are too weak or who have loose stools. During medication, raw, cold and indigestable food should be avoided.

4.1.3. Baby-soothing Pill

Indications: Emaciation, fever with irritability and fidget, dry skin and hair, restlessness in babies.

Prescription: Fructus Quisqualis (shelled) 10 Pcs, Rhizoma Picrorhizae 20g, Silicea Bambusae 20g, Ramulus Uncariae cum Uncis 20g, Periostracum Cicadae (feet removed, slightly stir-fried) 30 Pcs, Faeces Trogopterorum 26g, Cinnabaris (prepared with water) 20g.

Administration: Grind the above ingredients into a fine powder, make pills (as big as seeds of Chinese parasol tree) with processed honey coated with Cinnabaris. Babies below 1 year take half a pill, 1 year plus take 1~2 pills. The pills can be taken 2~3 times a day with millet gruel.

4.2. *Infantile Convulsion*

4.2.1. Powder for Treating Convulsion

Indications: Infantile convulsion with fever, spasm, clenched teeth and profuse phlegm.

Prescription: Gygsum Fibrosum 15g, Arisaema cum Bile 7.5g, Scorpio 4.5g, Periostracum Cicadae 4.5g, Scolopendra 4.5g, Silicea Bambusae 12g, Cinnabaris 6g, Aurum 5 sheets.

Administration: Grind the above ingredients into a fine powder and take 3 times a day with sugar and water. (Babies below

6 months take 0.1g, between 6 months and 1 year take 0.12~0.3g, 1 year plus 0.3~0.5g).

4.2.2. Powder for Expelling Wind Evil

Indications: Infantile convulsion caused by internal heat characterized by spasm of the four limbs, fixation of eyes, lockjaw, cough with profuse phlegm and constipation.

Prescription: Rhizoma Rhei 30g, Succinum 10g, Radix Curcumae 10g, Cinnabaris (prepared with water) 10g, Ramulus Uncariae cum Uncis 9g, Radix Scutellariae 9g, Radix Glycyrrhizae powder 15g.

Administration: Grind the above ingredients into a fine powder. Babies below 1 year take 0.2~0.3g, 1 year plus take 0.3~0.5g with sugar and water.

Note: Not to be administered to babies with loose stools.

4.2.3. Convulsion-preventing Powder

Indications: Infantile indigestion, abdominal distension with internal heat and restlessness with pale complexion indicating signs of convulsion.

Prescription: Defatted croton seed powder 6g, Bulbus Fritillariae Cirrhosae 4.5g, Radix Platycodi 4.5g, Radix Glycyrrhizae powder 3g.

Administration: Grind the above ingredients into a very fine powder and take once a day before eating, Babies between 6 months and 1 year take 0.1 ~ 0.25g. The dosage varies with age and constitution.

Note: As the drug is strongly purgative, babies of weak constitution should avoid taking it.

4.3. Neonatal Tetanus

4.3.1. Powder for Treating Neonatal Tetanus

Indications: Neonatal tetanus in newborn.

Prescription: Bombyx Batryticatus (baked brown) 1 Piece, Scorpio (baked brown) 1 Piece, Periostracum Cicadae (feet removed baked brown) 1 Piece.

Administration: Grind the 3 ingredients into a powder. Take 1/3 with honey once a day for 3 days. White saliva brought out after medication is a sign of effectiveness.

4.4. Morbid Night Crying of a Baby

4.4.1. Decoction for Stopping Night Crying Recipe I

Indications: Morbid night crying of a baby.

Prescription: Periostracum Cicadae (head and foot removed) 6 Pcs, Lumbricus (stir-fried) 1 Piece, Radix Linderae 2g, Poria 3g, Radix Glycyrrhizae 1g, Fructus Ziziphi Jujubae 1 Piece, Cinnabaris (prepared with water) 0.1g.

Administration: Make a decoction with the above ingredients. Take one dose per day.

Note: Clinical practice shows that 3~6 doses will surely bring about a cure.

4.4.2. Decoction for Stopping Night Crying Recipe II

Indications: Morbid night crying of a baby with convulsive seizures.

Prescription: Medulla Junci 2g, Terra Flava Usta 6g.

Administration: Decoct the Medulla Junci for 10 minutes and then put Terra Flava Usta into the decoction. Feed the baby with the clear liquid of the decoction.

4.5. Whooping Cough

4.5.1. Whooping Cough Oil

Indications: Whooping cough.

Prescription: Spiders 2 Pcs, curved thorns on the date tree 6 Pcs, Sesame oil 1 soupspoonful.

Administration: Fry the spiders and thorns in the sesame oil in a laddle with small fire. Remove the spiders and thorns when they dry up. Feed the baby with warm oil once a day.

Note: For babies below 1 year, 1 spider is enough.

4.5.2. Powder of Chicken Gallbladder and Radix Glycyrrhizae

Indications: Whooping cough.

Prescription: Chicken gallbladders 10 Pcs, Radix Glycyrrhizae (powdered) 10g, crystal sugar q. s.

Administration: Fresh chicken gallbladders are each added with Radix Glycyrrhizae powder to be dried up in the shade. Grind the dry gallbladders and crystal sugar into a powder and take it twice a day with sugar and water. Babies below 1 year take 0.2～0.3g each time, 1～3 years take 0.3～0.5g, 3～5 years 0.5～1g. The dosage varies with age.

4.5.3. Flos Genkwa Pill

Indications: Whooping cough.

Prescription: Flos Genkwa 20g, Radix Euphorbiae Kansui 20g, Radix Euphorbiae Pekinsensis 20g, Bombyx Batryticatus 15g, flour (stir-fried light brown) 100g.

Administration: Grind the ingredients into a powder and mix the powder well with the flour and processed honey to make pills as big as seeds of Chinese Parasol tree. Take the pills with water every morning. Babies between 1～2 years take 1 pill, 2～4 years 1.5～2 pills, 5 years plus 2～3 pills.

4.5.4. Cough-relieving Powder for Children

Indications: Cough, asthma in children induced by various causes.

Prescription: Carapax Trionycis (prepared) 15g, Semen pruni Armeniacae (stir-fried) 15g, Bulbus Fritillariae Cirrhosae 15g, Cortex Mori Radicis 15g, Radix Glycyrrhizae (powdered) 15g, Bulbus Lilli (prepared) 12g, Rhizoma Pinelliae 12g, Radix Stemonae 9g, Folium Perillae 9g, Radix Polygalae 9g, Pericarpium Citri Reticulatae 9g, Poria 9g, Bombyx Batryticatus (stir-fried) 9g, Cordyceps 9g, Gypsum Fibrosum 9g, Herba Menthae 6g, Radix Peucedani 6g, Semen Plantaginis (stir-fried) 6g, Semen Lipidii seu Descurainiae (stir-fried) 6g, Herba Asari 6g, Rhizoma Zingiberis 6g, Herba Ephedrae 3g.

Administration: Grind the above ingredients into a powder. Take it 3 times a day with water. Babies below 6 months cannot take more than 0.25g each time, between 6 months and 1 year not more than 0.5g, 1~6 years not more than 1g, 6~12 years not more than 1.5g.

4.6. Measles

4.6.1. Powder for Promoting Eruption of Measles

Indications: The beginning stage of measles which fail to erupt quickly complicated by fever, cough and restlessness.

Prescription: Flos Lonicerae 12g, Radix Ledebouriellae 12g, Radix Trichosanthis 12g, Fructus Forsythiae 18g, Semen Pruni Armeniacae 18g, Herba Menthae 9g, Radix Platycodi 9g, Herba Lophatheri 9g, Herba Schizonepetae 6g, Radix Glycyrrhizae 6g.

Administration: Grind the above ingredients into a fine powder. Take it 3 times per day with decoction of Herba Coriandri Sativi. Children below 1 year cannot take more than 0.3g each time, 3 years below not more than 0.6g, 6~12 years less than 1~1.5g.

Note: Decades of experience with this powder has shown that it is very effective when it is used properly.

4.6.2. Powder for Clearing Away Fever

Indications: Fever and measles in children.

Prescription: Cornu Bubali 30g, goat horn 20g, Talcum 20g, Calculus Bovis (synthetic) 15g, Flos Lonicerae 15g, Bulbus Fritillariae Cirrhosae 15g, Radix Trichosanthis 15g, Radix Scutellariae 15g, Radix et Rhizoma Rhei 15g, Fructus Aurantii 15g, Fructus Forsythiae 15g, Fructus Gardeniae 15g, Radix Glycyrrhizae 15g, Succinum 10g, Cinnabaris 10g, Radix Bupleuri 10g, Radix Sophorae Subprostratae 10g, Fructus Amomi Rotundus 12g, Rhizoma Coptidis 12g, Moschus 1.5g, Fructus Mume 3g.

Administration: First grind Calculus Bovis, Succinum, Moschus, Fructus Mume, Cinnabaris separately into powders, then grind the other ingredients together into a powder and mix all the powders together. Take 2~3 times a day with sugar and water. Children below 1 year take 0.3g each time, 1~3 years 0.5~1g, 3~6 years 1~1.5g.

4.6.3. Decoction for Promoting Eruption of Measles

Indications: Failure in full eruption of measles complicated with high fever.

Prescription: Mung beans 30g, Rhizoma Imperatae (fresh) 30g, Periostracum Cicadae 12 Pcs, Gypsum Fibrosum 9g, Herba Coriandri Sativi 3g.

Administration: Make a decoction with the above ingredients and take it frequently and finish the decoction in one day. The dosage varies according to age and severity.

4.7. Infantile Parasitosis

4.7.1. Decoction of Fructus Quisqualis and Cortex Meliae

Indications: Roundworm with occasional abdominal pain, vomiting and a mass in the abdomen.

Prescription: Fructus Quisqualis (one year one piece), Cortex Meliae (fresh) 15g, Fructus Mume (one year two pieces).

Administration: Make a decoction of the above ingredients and take half in the morning, half in the evening.

4.7.2. Pinworm-expelling Powder

Indications: Infantile oxyuriasis with itchy sensation in the anus, especially in the evening.

Prescription: Semen Torreyae (stir-fried) 5g, Semen Arecae (stir-fried) 30g, Omphalia 12g.

Administration: Grind the ingredients into a powder. Take it twice a day with water for 3 days. 5 years below take 1～1.5g each time, 5 years plus take 2～2.5g.

4.7.3. Pill of Green Vitriol and Fructus Quisqualis

Indications: Ancylostomiasis in children with food preference to earth, bricks, cinder, eggshell etc.

Prescription: Green vitriol 12g, Fructus Quisqualis 6g, Semen Arecae (burnt) 6g, Rhizoma Atractylodis Macrocephalae (burnt) 9g, Fructus Amomi 9g, Omphalia 3g, Pericarpium Citri Reticulatae 3g.

Administration: Grind the above ingredients into a fine powder and make pills as big as mung beans with boiling vinegar and the powder, then dry the pills for use. Children between 3～5 years take 6～10 pills, 6～10 years take 10～15 pills each time, twice a day.

Note: Tea should be avoided during administration. Generally

3~5 days of usage will show signs of improvement.

4.8. Infantile Diarrhea

4.8.1. Powder for Stopping Diarrhea

Indications: Intractable diarrhea in children due to deficiency of spleen.

Prescription: Semen Coicis (stir-fried) 12g, Rhizoma Dioscoreae (fresh) 12g, Poria 9g, Semen Euryales (stir-fried) 9g, Rhizoma Atractylodis Macrocephalae (burnt) 9g, Semen Plantaginis (stir-fried with wine) 9g, Semen Nelumbinis (stir-fried) 6g, Radix Paeoniae Alba (stir-fried with wine) 6g, Radix Glycyrrhizae 6g.

Administration: Grind the above ingredients into a fine powder. Take it 3 times a day with water. Children between 3 months to 1 year take 0.5~0.7g each time, 1~3 years take 0.7~1.2g, 3~6 years take 1.2~1.5g.

Note: During medication, raw, cold, oily and indigestable food should be avoided.

4.9. Infantile Abdominal Pain (Appendix: Abdominal Distension)

4.9.1. Powder for Abdominal Pain in Children

Indications: Abdominal pain in children caused by eating raw or cold food.

Prescription: Rhizoma Corydalis 30g, Fructus Piperis Longi 24g, Fructus Foeniculi (stir-fried) 24g, Radix Linderae 12g, Radix Glycyrrhizae 6g.

Administration: Grind the above ingredients into a fine powder. Take the powder 3 times a day after mixing it with brown sugar and boiling water. Children of 1~3 years take

0.3~0.5g, 3~6years take 0.5~0.8g each time.

Caution: Children suffering from abdominal pain complicated by fever and dry stools should not be administered. During medication, raw, cold and oily food should be avoided.

Appendix: Abdominal distension with constipation Recipe I: Caulis Allii Fistulosi (1 stalk) is pounded to get juice, add same amount of milk into the juice and feed the child with the mixture. Very soon there will be a bowel movement and the distension will disappear.

Recipe II: Peach tree leaves gathered in autumn q.s., are decocted for 2 hours. Then remove the residue and reheat the decoction until it turns into a semi-fluid extract. Make a plaster with some of the extract and a piece of cloth, apply the plaster to the navel after cleaning the navel with fresh ginger slices. The plaster should be changed once every 2 days. This recipe is for treating habitual abdominal distension in children.

4.10. *Prolapse of Rectum in Children*

4.10.1. Powder for Treating Prolapse of Rectum

Indications: Prolapse of rectum in children induced by long-standing diarrhea.

Prescription: Galla Chinensis 15g, Alumen 15g, Semen Momordicae 2 Pcs, Periostracum Cicadae 12 Pcs.

Administration: Grind the above ingredients into a very fine powder. Apply the powder to the prolapsed part after washing it, then push the affected part into its normal position.

Note: Years of clinical practice proves that at most 6 doses will bring about a cure.

4.10.2. Decoction of Radix Astragali seu Hedysari

Indications: Prolapse of rectum with deficency of spleen and qi.

Prescription: Radix Astragali seu Hedysari 12g, Rhizoma Astractylodis Macrocephalae (burnt) 6g, Fructus Mume 6g, Radix Paeoniae Rubra 3g, Fructus Aurantii 3g, Radix Ledebouriellae 3g, Rhizoma Cimicifugae 3g, Fructus Schisandrae 3g.

Administration: Make a decoction of the above ingredients and take half of the decoction in the morning, half in the evening.

4.11. Omphalelcosis
4.11.1. Powder for Treating Omphalelcosis

Indications: Discharge of liquid or pus of the umbilical cord in the newborn.

Prescription: Galla Chinensis (big) 1 Piece, silkworm cocoon 1 Piece.

Administration: Break a small hole on the Galla Chinensis, remove the dregs inside, and replace them with the cocoon. Then burn them and grind them into a powder. Apply the powder to the affected part.

4.12. Boil of the Chin in Children
4.12.1. Ointment of Carbonized Dates

Indications: Boil of the chin with yellow discharge in children.

Prescription: Fructus Ziziphi Jujubae (carbonized) q. s.

Administration: Grind the ingredient into a fine powder and mix it with sesame oil, apply the ointment once a day to the affected area after washing it with warm water.

4.13. Fetal Toxins

4.13.1. Ointment for Treating Fetal Toxins (Appendix)

Indications: Fetal Toxins.

Prescription: Alumen 6g, Nidus Vespae (carbonized) 1 Piece, old cotton (burnt) q. s., sesame oil q. s.

Administration: Grind the above ingredients and mix them with oil. Apply the ointment to the affected part once or twice a day.

Appendix: Exocarpium Citrulli (carbonized) 10g, Borax 10g and Borneolum Syntheticum 1g to be ground into a powder. Mix the powder with sesame oil and then apply to the affected part.

4.13.2. Decoction of Flos Trollii and Radix Rehmanniae

Indications: Fetal toxins.

Prescription: Flos Trollii 6g, Radix Rehmanniae 6g, Radix Trichosanthis 6g, Radix Glycyrrhizae (powdered) 6g.

Administration: Decoct the above ingredients. Take 1/3 of the decoction in the morning, 1/3 in the afternoon, 1/3 in the evening.

4.14. Mumps

4.14.1. Powder for Treating Mumps (Appendix)

Indications: Mumps.

Prescription: Borneolum Syntheticum 1g, Realgar 3g, Alumen 6g.

Administration: Grind the above ingredients into a fine powder. Make a paste with 1 stalk of pounded Caulis Allii Fistulosi and proper amount of egg white and the powder. Then apply the paste to the affected part.

Appendix: Cacumen Biotae, Herba Portulacae of the same amount. Pound and mix them with egg white. Apply the paste to the affected area and change the medicine once a day.

4.15. Heat Rash

4.15.1. Powder of Mung Bean and Talcum (Appendix)

Indications: Heat rash.

Prescription: Powder of mung bean and Talcum (equal amount).

Administration: First rub the affected place with juice from pounded towel gourd leaves, then spread the mixed powder over the place 1~2 times a day. 3~5 times will bring about a cure.

Appendix: Rub the affected place with a piece of ice 1~2 times a day, and the heat rash will disappear in 2 days.

5. Department of the Five-sense Organs

5.1. *Ophthalmology*

5.1.1. Sight-recovering Decoction

Indications: Nyctalopia.

Prescription: Rhizoma Atractylodis 15g, bat faeces 10g, fresh pork liver 100g, fresh mutton liver 100g, fresh chicken liver 1 Piece.

Administration: Boil the above ingredients till the livers are well done. Remove the first two ingredients and eat up the soup and livers in one day.

5.1.2. Nebula-expelling Decoction

Indications: Red nebula with swollen and red eyes.

Prescription: Folium Mori (frost-beaten) 12g, Flos Chrysanthemi 9g, Rhizoma Coptidis 9g, Chalcanthitus (Calcined) 1.5g, Semen pruni Armeniacae 2 Pcs.

Administration: Make a decoction of the above ingredients. Soak a clean towel in the hot clear liquid of the decoction. Use the towel as a hot compress on the eyes twice a day. 3 ~5 days will bring about a cure.

5.1.3. Nebula-expelling Powder

Indications: Nebula in the eyes, blurred vision.

Prescription: Concha Haliotidis, Resina Draconis, Commiphora Myrrha, Os Sepiellae seu Sepiae, Rhizoma Rhei,

Natrii Sulfas and Flos Chrysanthemi all of equal amount.

Administration: Grind the above ingredients into a fine powder. Take it twice a day, 10g each time with warm millet wine.

5.1.4. Trichiasis-adjusting Ointment

Indications: Trichiasis.

Prescription: Galla Chinensis 50g, honey q. s.

Administration: Cut the galls open to remove the dregs inside, then grind them into a very fine powder and mix the powder with honey. Apply the ointment to the affected eyelid twice a day.

5.2. *Otopathy*

5.2.1. Powder of Cow Gallbladder and Mung Beans

Indications: Suppurative otitis media.

Prescription: Cow gallbladder 1 Piece, mung beans q.s.

Administration: First wash the fat off the gallbladder, then fill the gallbladder with mung beans and tie the opening with a string. Then dry it in the shade. Afterwards bake the dry gall light brown and grind it into a powder. For application, wash the ear with hydrogen peroxide solution, then blow a tiny portion of powder into the ear 1~2 times a day.

Note: Clinical experience shows that 3~4 times of application of the powder will bring about a cure.

5.3. *Rhinitis*

5.3.1. Semi-fluid Extract for Treating Rhinitis

Indications: Chronic rhinitis.

Prescription: Fructus Xanthii (pounded) 1500g, Flos Magnoliae 600g, Fructus Viticis 600g, Radix Angelicae Dahuricae 500g, moss on shaded side of wall 150g.

Administration: Put the above ingredients into an ironpot, add 12 litre of water and stew it for 3 hours, filter the decoction with a piece of gauze, stew the decoction again until 3 litre is left. Then add honey 1000 ml and boil 10 minutes more. Store the semi-fluid extract in an earthenware jar and take one soupspoonful of it 3 times a day with water. Generally the patient will recover when he has finished taking the whole extract.

5.3.2. Powder for Treating Rhinitis

Indications: Chronic rhinitis.

Prescription: Flos Syzygii Aromatici (stir-fried brown) 6g, moss on the shaded side of wall (washed and dried in the shade) 9g, Rhizoma Coptidis (stir-fried light brown) 2g, Borneolum Syntheticum 0.2g.

Administration: Grind the first three ingredients into a powder then add Borneolum Syntheticum and grind again into a fine powder. Take out a tiny portion (like a husked sorghum in size) and inhale the powder directly into the nostrils twice a day.

5.4. Sore Throat

5.4.1. Sore Throat Drink

Indications: Sore throat with hoarse voice.

Prescription: Semen Sterculiae Scaphigerae 2 Pcs, Radix Ophiopogonis 4g, Radix Platycodi 4g, Flos Lonicerae 2g, Radix Glycyrrhizae 3g.

Administration: Put the above ingredients and some sugar into a teapot, then pour into it boiling water and drink the liquid like tea. Change fresh ingredients once a day.

5.4.2. Powder for Pharyngitis

Indications: Sore throat with difficulty in swallowing due to acute or chronic pharyngitis.

Prescription: Bulbus Fritillariae Cirrhosae 12g, Radix Sophorae Subprostratae 6g, Alumen 3g, Borax 3g, Fructus Mume 0.5g.

Administration: Grind the above ingredients into a fine powder, blow a tiny portion of it into the throat or suck a little and swallow slowly 2~3 times a day.

5.4.3. Powder for Throat Ailments

Indications: All sorts of throat ailments.

prescription: Rhizoma Coptidis 25g, Bombyx Batryticatus 25g, Borax 25g, Alumen 25g, Natrii Sulfas 25g, Sal Nitri 25g, Indigo Naturalis 25g, Herba Menthae 25g.

Administration: Grind the above ingredients into a fine powder and mix it with the bile from a male pig killed in January. Put the mixture back into the gallbladder and tie the opening with a string, then put the bladder into an earthenware jar and bury it 0.67m deep in the shade on the day of Great Cold (24th solor term), and unearth it on the seconded day of the beginning of Spring (1st solar term). Now dry the gall bladder in the shade and take out the dry mass from the bladder and grind it into a fine powder with Borneolum Syntheticum 2g, Moschus 1g and Margarita (powder) 0.5g. Store the powder in a porcelain jar (sealed). For Application, blow a bit powder into the throat 7~8 times a day, or suck a little to swallow slowly.

Note: The recipe was handed down from older generations of the family, the process in making the drug should be strictly followed. Years of application with this recipe proves its fast and sustaining effect on throat ailments.

5.4.4. Voice-recovering Drink
Indications: Hoarse voice.

Prescription: Bark of an old white poplar (stir-fried) 12g, Herba pteridis Miltifidae (stir-fried) 10g, Radix Ophiopogonis 4g.

Administration: Make a decoction of the above ingredients and take the whole decoction once a day for 3 days. Or pour boiling water into the ingredients and drink the liquid like tea.

5.5. Mouth Cavity Ailment

5.5.1. Powder of Fructus Euodiae and Water-melon Frost
Indications: Mouth sore.

Prescription: Fructus Euodiae 6g, powder on the surface of a dried persimmon 3g, water-melon frost 3g, Borneolum Syntheticum 0.2g.

Administration: Grind the above ingredients into a fine powder and apply a tiny portion of the powder to the affected place twice a day.

5.5.2. Ache-relieving Powder
Indications: Toothache, headache.

Prescription: Rhizoma Ligustici Chuanxiong 6g, Gypsum Fibrosum 6g, Resina Boswelliae Carterii (prepared) 2g, Commiphora Myrrha (prepared) 2g, Radix Angelicae Dahuricae 3g, Realgar 4.5g, Sal Nitri 9g.

Administration: Grind the above ingredients into a powder and inhale a tiny amount into the nostrils, the ache will be relieved instantly.

Note: Do not inhale too much or too frequently, in case the

powder stimulates the nostrils and causes discomfort in nasal cavity.

5.5.3. Colophonium Paste

Indications: Toothaches resulted from various causes.

Prescription: Colophonium 20g, Borneolum Syntheticum 1g.

Administration: First pound Colophonium, then add Borneolum Syntheticum and grind them together into a fine powder. Now spread the powder 3 mm thick over a piece of oval-shaped white cloth, pour drops of white wine onto the powder until it is soaked through. Apply the plaster to the affected area on the face and change the plaster once a day or once every two days.

Note: Clinical practice shows that the plaster works well with all sorts of toothaches. Generally 1 ~ 2 plasters will bring about a cure.

5.5.4. Quick-acting Powder for Toothache

Indications: Toothache due to attack of wind-fire.

Prescription: Herba Asari 4.5g, Cortex Cinnamomi 3g, Rhizoma Alpiniae officinarum 5g, Herba Menthae (crystalized) 4g, Borneolum Syntheticum 0.5g.

Administration: Grind the first 3 ingredients into a powder, then add the rest for further grinding. Store the powder in a porcelain bottle and seal it well. For application, inhale a little powder into a nostril. (For toothache on the left, inhale it with the right nostril, for the right side toothache, inhale it with the left one) An immediate effect will be felt.

5.5.5. Ten Ingredients Decoction for Treating Toothache

Indications: Intractable toothache.

Prescription: Radix Aconiti 6g, Radix Aconiti Kusnezoffii 6g, Radix et Rhizoma Rhei 6g, Radix Angelicae Pubescentis 6g,

Radix Angelicae Dahuricae 9g, Radix Scrophulariae 9g, Radix Rehmanniae 12g, Herba Asari 3g, Rhizoma Cimicifugae 10g, Gypsum Fibrosum 15g.

Administration: Make a decoction of the above ingredients and take half of the decoction in the morning, half in the evening.

6. Others

6.1. Medicinal Wine for Trauma

Indications: Traumatic injury with reddness and swelling, fracture of bones.

Prescription: Radix Codonopsis Pilosulae 24g, Caulis Spatholobi 24g, Radix Polygoni Multiflori 24g, Fructus Lycii 24g, Radix Aconiti Kusnezoffii 12g, Radix Rubiae 12g, Radix Angelicae Sinensis 12g, Radix Paeoniae Alba 12g, Fructus Chaenomelis 12g, Rhizoma Ligustici Chuanxiong 6g, Resina Boswelliae Carterii 6g, Commiphora Myrrha 6g, white wine 1000g.

Administration: Soak the above ingredients in the wine for 7 days. Apply the medicated wine to the affected place with a piece of absorbent cotton 3 times a day. In the case of severe injury or bone fracture, the cotton absorbed with wine may be left on the affected area with a dressing which is removed in 2 hours. The cotton may be applied 3~4 times a day or more frequently in accordance with the severity of cases.

Caution: The wine is not to be taken by mouth, nor can it be in contact with open cut in the skin.

6.2. Black Plaster

Indications: Numbness due to wind-cold invasion, pain in the legs and waist, acute cervical lymphadenitis.

Prescription: Radix Angelicae Sinensis 6g, Rhizoma Ligustici Chuanxiong 6g, Flos Carthami 6g, Herba Ephedrae 6g, Radix Ledebouriellae 6g, Cortex Eucommiae 6g, Radix Dipsaci 6g, Radix Gentianae Macrophyllae 6g, Herba Schizonepetae 6g, Ramulus Cinnamomi 6g, Radix Stephaniae Tetrandrae 6g, Radix Aconiti 6g, Fructus Chaenomelis 6g, Radix Aconiti Kusnezoffii 6g, Cortex Illicii 6g, Rhizoma Homalomenae 6g, Catechu 6g, Resina Boswelliae Carterii 6g, Commiphora Myrrha 6g, Radix Cyathulae 6g, Radix Clematidis 6g, Squama Manitis 6g, Semen Momordicae 6g, Resina Draconis 6g, 2 frogs, some hair, sesame oil 750g, Minium (to be added late) 160g.

Administration; Soak the ingredients (not including Minium) in the sesame oil for two days, then fry them on a small fire until they dry up, remove the dregs and stew on fire till a drop poured out forms a ball, then add Minium slowly while stirring the mixture, heat again on fire until big bubbles almost disappear. Finally pour the mixture into water and change water once a day for 7 days. For application, melt the mixture and put some on a piece of cloth to make a plaster, then apply the plaster to the affected place. Change the plaster once every 10 days.

6.3. *Resuscitation Powder*

Indications: Summer heat, high fever with convulsion and coma (analogous to epedemic encephalitis B in modern medicine).

Prescription: Cow-bezoar Powder for Resurrection, Purple Snowy Powder, Treasured Bolus, Powder of Calculus Macacae Mulattae and Powder of Radix Ginseng all of equal amount.

Administration: Grind the above ingredients into a very fine powder which can be taken accordingly after mixing it with the decoction of Herba Lophatheri. In the case of unconsciousness, the drug may be given through nose once every 3 ~4 hours.

6.4. Nightmare-Expelling Decoction

Indications: Nightmare with palpitation and fright.

Prescription: Rhizoma Rehmanniae Praparatae 20g, Fructus Lycii 20g, Fructus Ligustrilucidi 20g, Os Draconis 20g, Concha Ostreae 20g, Radix Polygoni Multiflori 15g, Semen Ziziphi Spinosae (stir-fried) 15g, Concha Margaritifera Usta 15g, Radix Glycyrrhizae (powdered) 12g, Poria 12g, Fructus Schisandrae 12g, Radix Polygalae 10g, Rhizoma Acori Graminel 10g, Colla Cornus Cervi 10g.

Administration: Decoct 3 times the above ingredients and put the decoctions together. Take 1/3 in the morning, 1/3 in the afternoon and 1/3 in the evening.

Note: During medication, raw and cold food, vexation and sex should be avoided.

6.5. Sleeping Decoction

Indications: Insomnia, restlessness.

Prescription: Plumula Nelumbinis 9g, Radix Rehmanniae 9g, Semen Caesalpiniae 10g, Radix Ophiopogonis 10g, Bulbus Lilii 10g, Fructus Gardeniae 10g, Fructus Forsythiae 10g, Cortex Albiziae 10g, Bamboo Leaves 6g, Caulis Bambusae in Taeniam 6g, Radix Glycyrrhizae 6g.

Administration: Decoct the above ingredients twice and put the decoctions together. Take half of the volume in the morning, half in the evening with empty stomach.

6.6. Wonder Pill

Indications: Mania (Schizophrenia).

Prescription: Radix Euphorbiae Kansui 10g, Radix Knoxiae 10g, Cinnabaris (prepared with water) 10g, Semen Sinapis Albae 10g, Curcuma Kwangsiensis 10g, Lignum Aquilariae Resinatum 10g, Calculus Bovis 0.5g, Borneolum Syntheticum 0.5g.

Administration: Grind the first 6 ingredients into a fine powder, then add the rest two ingredients for further grinding. Mix the powder with processed honey to make pills of 1g each. The dosage varies from $1 \sim 3$ pills each time according to the severity of illness and constitution of the patient. The pill should be taken twice a day with water.

6.7. Pill of Strychni and Lumbricus

Indications: Epilepsy.

Prescription: Semen Strychni (boiled and then hair removed, afterwards fried in the sesame oil) 50g, Lumbricus 50g, Scolopendra 10 Pcs, Arisaema cum Bile 10g, Radix Ginseng 30g, Rhizoma Typhonii 10g.

Administration: Grind the above ingredients into a fine powder and mix it with processed honey to make pills as big as seeds of Chinese parasol tree. Take 3 pills before sleep the first day, then add one more pill each evening until a tightness and numbness sensation is felt around the teeth (usually when the dosage is increased to $7 \sim 8$ pills), then keep a steady dose.

6.8. Spider Ointment

Indications: Thromboangiitis obliterans.

Prescription: Big spiders (with 7 stars on the back) 7 Pcs, Resina Draconis 10g, Natrii Sulfas 6g, Resina Boswelliae Carterii 5g, Crinis Carbonisatus 5g, Borneolum Syntheticum 1g, Cera Flava 20g, sesame oil 100g.

Administration: Pound the above ingredients (excluding Cera Flava) into a paste, stew the oil to semi-fluid, then add the paste to the oil for further stewing. After a while turn off the fire and add Cera Flava to the mixture while stirring them well. When the Ointment cools down, store it in a porcelain jar. For application, make a plaster with a piece of cloth (the size of which should be in accordance with the size of the affected area) and the Ointment. Change the plaster once a day.

6.9. Bolus for Treating Consumption

Indications: Lung consumption (T. B.) with symptoms like cough, spitting blood-mixed phlegm, dyspnea, discomfort around the costal regions.

Prescription: Fructus Gardeniae, Rhizoma Bletillae, Pericarpium Citri Reticulatae, Semen Arecae, Radix Platycodi, Bulbus Fritillariae Cirrhosae, Radix Glycyrrhizae all of equal amount.

Administration: Grind them together into a fine powder and mix it with processed honey to make boluses of 10g each, Take 1 bolus twice a day before eating with brown sugar 30g and water.

6.10. Pain-relieving Powder

Indications: Mobile pain in the body like being drilled, occurring recently or for a long time.

Prescription: Endothelium Corneum Gigeriae Galli 50g, Semen Phaseoli 50g, Rhizoma Zingiberis 50g, Placenta powder 50g, Cicada Nymph (wings removed) 9 Pcs, Cinnabaris 10g.

Administration: Grind the Cinnabaris separately and prepare it with water. Then grind the rest together into a fine powder and mix the two powders. For application, take 10g twice a day after breakfast and supper with sugar and water for male patients, brown sugar and water for female patients. Pain will disappear after days of treatment.

6.11. Stye-Dispersing Paste

Indications: Stye.

Prescription: Galla Chinensis 10g, Rhizoma Pinelliae 10g, Rhizoma Arisaematis 10g, Borneolum Syntheticum 1g.

Administration: Grind the above ingredients into a fine powder, make a paste with vinegar and apply the paste to the affected place before sleep.

6.12. Pain-Relieving Decoction

Indications: Sudden sprain in the lumbar region with feeling of pain in the chest when breathing, pain in the lumbar and costal regions.

Prescription: Radix Angelicae Sinensis 10g, Radix Paeoniae Rubra 9g, Semen Persicae (stir-fried) 9g, Radix Dipsaci 9g, Herba Lycopi 9g, Cortex Eucommiae (carbonized)

9g, Resina Boswelliae Carterii (prepared) 6g, Commiphora Myrrha (prepared) 6g, Radix Saussureae Lappae 6g, Fructus Foeniculi 6g, Radix Glycyrrhizae 6g.

Administration: Decoct the above ingredients twice and put the decoctions together. Take half of the volume in the morning, half in the evening. Generally, 2~4 doses will bring about a cure.

6.13. *Semen Lotion*

Indications: Intractable skin disease on the face manifested as red boils.

Preseription: Semen Hydnocarpi 9g, Fructus Cannabis 9g, Semen Juglandis 9g, Semen Momordicae 6g, Camphora 6g, Hydrargyrum 9g.

Administration: Pound the above ingredients in a new earthenware utensil into a paste, then wrap the paste with a piece of white cloth and the oily substance which oozes out of the cloth is applied to the affected face twice a day. Generally 20 days of use will show signs of improvement, and 45 days (when the lotion is used up) will bring about a cure. (Cover the utensil well after applications).

Caution: Be cautious not to contact mouth, as it is poisonous.

6.14. *Plaster for Hyperplasia of Bones*

Indications: Hyperplasia of bones leading to pain of the legs and waist.

Prescription: Radix Knoxiae 30g, Herba Dendrobii 30g, Rhizoma Coptidis 30g, Radix Scrophulariae 30g, Herba Incarvilleae Sinensis 30g, Semen Momordicae 30g, Radix Ledebouriellae 30g, Resina Boswelliae Carterii 30g, Commiphora Myrrha 30g, Radix Angelicae Pubescentis 30g, Fructus Gleditsiae Abnormalis 36g, Radix Angelicae Dahuricae 36g, Rhizoma seu Radix Nota-Pterygii 36g, Radix Angelicae Sinensis 36g, Cortex Cinnamomi 36g, Rhizoma Sparganii 45g, Squama Manitis 45g, Radix Rehmanniae 45g, Ramulus Cinnamomi 45g, Scorpio 45g, Os Tigris 60g, Rhizoma Bletillae 15g, Semen Hydnocarpi 15g, Radix Clematidis 15g, Fructus Aurantii Immaturus 15g, twigs of Chinese scholartree 15g, of elm tree 15g, of peach tree 15g, of willow tree 15g, Radix Sophorae Flavescentis 15g, Scolopendra 12 Pcs, Ancistrodon acutus 6 Pcs, Resina Draconis 50g, Radix Saussureae Lappae 25g, Rhizoma Gastrodiae 25g, Flos Carthami 25g, Herba Ephedrae 25g, Cortex Eucommiae 25g, Radix Paeoniae Rubra 25g, Moschus 12g, Lignum Santali 14g, Flos Caryophyllii 10g, Lithargyrum 120g.

Administration: When the 43 ingredients are made up, put aside 7 of them: Resina Draconis, Cortex Cinnamoni, Moschus, Flos Caryophyllii, Resina Boswelliae Carterii, Commiphora Myrrha and Lithargyrum. The other 36 ingredients are cut to small pieces and soaked in 4000g of sesame oil for 3 days. Then fry them until they are dried up, remove the dregs and heat the oil till it becomes a semi-fluid. Now turn off the fire and add Minium into the oil (for every 100g of oil 36g of Minium is added). Soak the ointment in the cold water for 10~15 days, then melt it and add the powder made from the 7 ingredients into the ointment and keep stirring to mix them well. For application, make a plaster with a piece of cloth and the ointment and put it on the affected area. Change the plaster every 20~30 days.

113

中国经效验方

谭凤华　谭凤森　谭弘慧　整理
杨慧琴　崔晓红　译
顿·沃尔特　审校
中国山东科学技术出版社出版
（中国济南玉函路 16 号）
外文印刷厂印刷
中国国际图书贸易总公司发行
（中国北京车公庄西路 35 号）
北京邮政信箱第 399 号　邮政编码 100044
1996 年第 1 版　　第 1 次印刷（英）
ISBN　7—5331—1630—5（外）
02400